Gift of Grace

Gift of Grace

Christian Inspirations

Regina McIntosh
Foreword by Brian Blankenship

RESOURCE *Publications* · Eugene, Oregon

GIFT OF GRACE
Christian Inspirations

Copyright © 2022 Regina McIntosh. All rights reserved. Except for brief quotations in critical publications or reviews, no part of this book may be reproduced in any manner without prior written permission from the publisher. Write: Permissions, Wipf and Stock Publishers, 199 W. 8th Ave., Suite 3, Eugene, OR 97401.

Resource Publications
An Imprint of Wipf and Stock Publishers
199 W. 8th Ave., Suite 3
Eugene, OR 97401

www.wipfandstock.com

PAPERBACK ISBN: 978-1-6667-4111-7
HARDCOVER ISBN: 978-1-6667-4112-4
EBOOK ISBN: 978-1-6667-4113-1

07/11/22

I would like to dedicate this "Gift of Grace" to my Lord and Savior, Jesus—the light of my spirit, the One who holds my heart, the maker of my soul, the joy that lives inside. Without Him, I wouldn't know what it is to feel the grace that He has rained down over my heart and soul, the wonder that abides in the prayers that make me whole, the saving grace that brings me to His cross again and again—In prayer and praise, I come to Him completely sure that He will always be there. He will always care. He will always share with me the intimacy of a friendship that is beyond compare. I love Him with my whole being and I can't wait to finally see Him face to face and thank Him for His "Gift of Grace"!

My heart's prayer is that someone out there will read something within these pages that will not allow them to turn away from the One who brightens lives and heals souls, the One who forgives to the uttermost, the One who died so that we could all know the intimacy with God that is even closer than the love of a child and a Father. He is a big, big God and I'm so very thankful that He chose to give us One who makes eternity with Him a option. If you're reading this and haven't felt the power of His love poured out across your soul, find a way to pray and make Him yours today! Read the enclosed Foreword for direction on discovering this "Gift of Grace" for yourself.

Contents

Foreword by Brian Blankenship | *xiii*
A Sinner's Prayer | *xiv*
Gift of Grace | 1
Hallelujah! Hallelujah!! | 3
Wisdom | 5
Song of the Soul | 8
Faith | 10
He is the wonder of my life | 12
Pax vobiscum | 13
Enoch Walked with God | 14
A Hard Heart | 15
Jesus, Use Me | 17
Take It to Jesus | 19
There Are Days When I Just Can't Pray | 21
God Is Always Good | 23
Believe | 25
A Simple Faith | 26
He Is GOD | 28
Jesus Himself | 30
Our Greatest Need | 32

In This Moment | 34
Eternal Life | 36
His Light | 38
Praising The King | 41
Dare to Believe | 43
Some Days | 45
God's Muse | 47
Life's Echo in Hell | 49
Eternally Grateful | 51
Praise Him | 54
What Love Isn't | 56
You Are ALIVE! | 58
Lead Me On | 60
To Him I Will Cling | 62
In Her Garden | 63
Beneath Her Tears | 65
Happy Easter Day | 67
Sonshine | 69
Good Friday | 71
Wilderness Prayers | 73
Forever and Always | 75
Blessings | 76
Freedom in Christ | 78
The Best Blessing | 79
Baptized into Hope | 80
I'll Follow Him | 82
Fear of the Lord | 83

Loving God | 85
The Comforter | 87
Prayer Warrior | 89
I Am the Clay | 90
Everlasting Love | 91
God's Child | 93
On the Inside | 95
Reflective Soul | 96
Just Believe | 98
Your Gift | 100
I Want Him to Know Me | 102
Fig Leaf | 104
A Simple Prayer | 106
He Is My Everything | 108
God of Angel Armies | 110
But God | 112
Forever Flying | 114
I Am Weak, But He Is Strong | 116
Godly Women | 118
The Final Journey | 120
Everyday, in Every Way | 122
Knowing God | 124
Joy in the Morning | 126
Holy Spirit Fire | 127
Hope Inspires | 129
Camping with Jesus | 131
Inside My Soul | 133

A Christian Thank You | 135
Relentless Love | 137
War's Words | 139
Secreted in the Scriptures | 141
He Is a Guiding Light | 143
His Entire Life | 145
Love So Alive | 147
In a Silent Prayer | 149
Fear Not | 151
The Light of Friendship | 152
Love Letter | 154
I Love Him | 156
He Is Worthy | 158
Keeper of the Flame | 160
World Peace | 161
He Is Alive | 163
With Prayer | 165
Saved by Grace | 167
God's Child | 170
I Yearn to Know Him | 172
Shine Down Your Love | 174
Redeeming Love | 176
When I Pray | 177
The Rudiments of Wings | 178
My God, My F O R E V E R | 180
Vein of Prayer | 182
Thankful for Grace | 183

He B L E S S E D Me | 185
The Night Sky | 187
The Savior of the World | 189
In the Moments | 192
Silent Prayers | 194
I'm Not a Very Good Christian | 195
A Humble Heart | 197
Glorious Savior | 199
Wonder of Wonders | 201
Reach for the Peace | 203
With Love Always | 205
My Father | 208
Living Proof | 210
You Are the Answer | 211
A Heavenly Home | 214
The Notebook | 215
Nothing but Blue Skies | 216
Autumn Years | 217
Lord, Please Help Me | 219
My Collections | 221
A Letter to God | 223
Holy Spirit | 225
Grief That Won't Let You Go | 227
His Guiding Light | 229
He Came for Us | 231
Change | 233
Walking His Path | 235

Foreword

Growing up in a small town in the Western North Carolina mountains, otherwise known as the "Bible Belt", has been one of my many great blessings. The biggest blessing I've had in my life is the good Christian daddy and mama that raised me in church, and with that, the seed was planted within me. "How did I get saved", you ask?

It was on an evening during one of our annual Bible Schools, June 14, 1993 to be exact. I didn't go to Bible School planning on getting saved. I went as a thirteen year old boy going to have fun with my friends. I wasn't looking for God, but by the grace of God his spirit came down in the midst of all my friends, and he found me. That evening I gave my heart and soul to Jesus Christ, God's son, the one who suffered and died on the cross for yours and my sins. He gave us the opportunity to be able to enter the kingdom of Heaven.

People will tell you that you can be saved in many different ways. I'm here to tell you that there is only one way, and that is by the grace of God. The Plan of Salvation: starts with acknowledging God as the creator of all things, and to accept your humble position in God's creation. Revelation 4:11 KJV Next, we all have to realize that we are all sinners and come short of the glory of God, Romans 3:23 KJV, and realize the wages of sin is death, Romans 6:23 KJV. God loved each and everyone of us that he sent his only begotten son, Jesus, to bear our sins and die in our place, Romans 5:8 KJV. It is very clear in the Bible, believe in Jesus as the one who bore your sins, died in your place, was buried, and whom God resurrected. It's Christ's blood and resurrection that assures us of everlasting life when we call on him as our Lord and Savior. For whosoever shall call upon the name of the Lord shall be saved. Romans 10:13 KJV. God loves us all. He did all this for me through his love as well as he would do it for you. I believe this to be true. I am now forty one years of age, and I have only truly known him for the past twenty eight years.

For the past sixteen years, I have delivered his messages to those in need. I pastor one of the little churches here in my area, and believe me when I say, how amazing the journey has been to see God work in people's lives. Regina resides in the same small town as I, and I have seen what God has done in her life. As you read in some of her poems, she is also familiar with GOD'S GRACE. And he said unto me, my grace is sufficient for thee: for my strength is made perfect in weakness. Most gladly therefore will I rather glory in my infirmities, that the power of Christ may rest upon me. 2 Corinthians 12:9 KJV.

Brian Blankenship
Pastor of Laurel Valley Baptist Church

A Sinner's Prayer

Oh Lord, Oh God, I am so sorry. Forgive me Lord, my dear sweet Heavenly Father. I realize now Lord of what I am. My heart hurts Lord. I am in pain. Please Lord I am at your mercy. I have heard of your Grace everlasting. I know now Lord that I need salvation. I beg you Lord to save me with your Grace. I know in surety that you are real Lord and I believe. Oh my God, I do believe. I feel your presence Lord, and I have a feeling in my heart Lord that I have never felt before. Lord, I cry, but it's a happiness I haven't ever quite felt—Oh Lord, my Lord, the weight is lifted off of me. I feel peace. Never have I quite felt the peace I feel within my soul. Oh Lord, oh my Heavenly Father, I feel I can live now and everything is going to be alright. Thank you Lord for sending your son to die on the cross. I know now because I can feel how much he loves me and why he died for all mankind. Lord this is new to me, a sinner saved by your Grace, but help me in this walk of life Lord because I know within myself I will fail. I know hardships will still come, but I don't have to walk alone. The greatest thing Lord is when my time comes, I can walk with you into the Kingdom of Heaven. Oh, thank you Lord, thank you Lord for knocking on my hearts door and giving me this chance. In Jesus's name, Amen.

Gift of Grace

Light falls soft against my heart
Pouring joy through my soul
Preparing me to give with a love
That is more alive than the thought
Who breathes a prayer, a plea
For hope that leaves a heart freed
From darkness, despair and dread
Feelings that erase happiness
With a shadow of pain and grief
Coloring dreams in disbelief

Light pours out its wispy warmth
Beckoning to my heart, shining
Into the soul who knows He brings
Assurance to the discouraged
Illumination to the depressed
Enlightenment to the distressed
He guides hearts into hopefulness
Sends peace to those who fear
Reminds the silence to sing again
With a love that frees the heart
He fills the mind with gentleness
A tender moment of kindness
Inspiration for all that brings
Wonder to those who praise Him

Light flows down from heaven above
Shimmering with blushing affections
Rising on the Son who is the pure love
Brought alive by His miraculous acceptance
Breathless inspiration cries to the soul
Who knows that God is always in control
He brings the heart a promise of beauty
Only found by the one who listens, eager

To glide into a dazzling dance, a waltz
Of laughter, lasting through the hesitation
From a heart who knows that this gift
Comes from the One who brings us love

This gift of grace is the answer to a prayer
Sent up from a heart who is crying out
For the One who reconciles us to our Father
Brings us an inspiration, a love, like no other!

Hallelujah! Hallelujah!!

I'm seeking God's will
For everything, each idea, every dream
I'm pursuing the Prince of peace,
The King of kings, the Wonder of wonders
Who created me and gave to me
The sweetest grace, the beauty of faith
Forgiveness and mercy, a second chance
To breath easy, knowing that He is
Alive, my risen Savior . . .

Someday, someway . . . He's coming back
To bring His children home to heaven
Where we will all be of one accord,
Filled with hope, faith and love . . . praising
The One who gave us His Son,
His Gift of Grace is salvation, redemption
A new birth—a new heart, a new home
Up in the sky where we will all fly
And where we will never die

I'm seeking God's will
For the brighter day, the best way, when I pray
I'm pursuing the gentle, tender faith,
The second chance, the kindest Redeemer,
Because I'm a believer who knows He is . . .
The only way toward unending grace
Mercy and peace, the beauty of devotion
Who lasts forever, the miracle of a Savior
Who makes a way where no way has been before
A Savior who I praise with my whole heart

Someday, someway—when He comes in the air
In the twinkling of an eye, we will find
. . . the answer to our prayers, His love

Has opened the door to a new world, a new hope
The beauty of light that has no shadow, no doubt
It is a light of love that never darkens, never goes out

Someday, someway—I will reach that home on high
Where there will be no tears—I won't ever cry
Where there will be no fears—I won't ever sigh
Where there will be only years—of joy and light
Love that comes alive, dancing across the heavens
To the music of His beauty, His grace, His embrace

Someday, someway—I will know His abiding peace
Will always be—never leaving me without a hope
Always there to help me to cope and assure my heart
That His love is the only way to truly know the wonder
Of heaven where my soul will never dread or despair
There will only be light that stirs to life our pleasure
Our elation and worship, our praise and admiration
Of a love that is more than breathtaking.
It is remarkable, humbling, spectacular.. it is love
That rouses the stars, the moon and sun . . . the heart
To believe that heaven is a home worthy of our adoration.

Someday, someway—Jesus will lift our spirits to a home
Where we will never want for anything, where we will never doubt
A home where our heart and soul will always worship Him—eternally
Giving God all the praise and thanks! Hallelujah! Hallelujah!!

Wisdom

> She is more precious than rubies; and all the things thou canst desire are not to be compared unto her.
> —PROVERBS 3:15

A golden glow
Fell from her heart
Shadowing dreams
In inspiration and hope
Reaching beyond
This sad, dark world
Into the promise
Of a heaven above

A beautiful peace
Cast laughter and faith
All around the ones
Who listened to her prayers
Litanies of wonder
Pleas for the yonder
When we would all know
What it is to believe
Beyond the idea
Into everlasting serenity

A soft breath of grace
Calming as the embrace
Of silence so gentle
It leaves vibrant colors
Halos of joy dancing
With the stars, the moon
Into the night where we know
The music that bleeds

Creativity, belief—her song
Felt by the soul, shimmering
With promises, imagination
Laughter that awakens
Assurance and inspiration

A silent tear kisses
Her smile, her light
Falling like a gentle rain
In pools of feeling
Flowing like the rivers
Soundless except for the sound
Of praise that sings
On the rapids as they move
Over smooth stones
Releasing the wonder
In her song

A breath of love
Lifted on the wind
Listening for the whispers
Of a lost light, a reflection
Mysterious shadows, a mist
Fading into her gaze
Of inspiration and grace
Musings of astonishment
Fading into the starlight
Shimmering across the sea
Beckoning for tender kisses
The embrace of His blessings
Remembering to reveal
An affection, feeling, passion
Adoration so very real
It appeals to the longings
Even the lonely can understand

Her silence reassures
Kindles rays of sunny thoughts
Reminders of this light, this love
That inspires, excites, stirs up
A desire to bring joy and hope
From the sorrow, worry and pain
A desire to give serenity and faith
To the heart who has been so afraid
The one who has lost their way
The soul who needs a second chance

Insight follows her path
With understanding and intuition
Her promise gives hope to the hopeless
Faith to the one who can't believe
And love to those with a fear
Of such a wonderful gift

With her, you can finally be sure
That the truth will be known
And you can find your way to weep
Tears of joy—as they spread
Anticipation to your wildest dreams!

Just trust her and she will forever be
Your best friend, your confidant
The light from your very prayers
Keep praying for her to embrace you
As God breaks through your spirit
Stirring you to give and give freely!

Song of the Soul

Merciful and wise, filled with light
My heavenly Father shines down
Coloring my soul in hues of compassion
A gentle flow of hope and faith
Inspiration that hallows my world

Tender and enlightened, His grace
Sheds light on my imagination, my praise
Glorifying His name, His way, His Son
With music and song, a dance of joy
Alive with roses and birds, butterflies
Wings of serenity, serving the earth
Like the moon and stars and sun as they
Rise, shimmer and stun our dreams
Into living out a feeling, a belief, a need
Swaying every thought, inspiring peace
His love is like the purity of a soul freed
By the One who left paradise to deliver
Our souls from sin that held them captive

Generous and gracious, His wisdom brings me
Unadulterated courage, strength and ambition
A second chance, a way to reach beyond faults
Into the penetrating warmth of a gentle thought
A heart and soul, both authentic and trustworthy
Dancing with kindness, liveliness, vibrancy
A feeling, a sparkle, a energy—resilient
Spiritually wise and willing to give to me
The proof that God is good and He is just
He gives sincerity and serenity and sensitivity
He fills the heart and soul with charity
A giving spirit of love, laughter—light
That brightens every thought and enlightens
Every hope . . . shimmering with insight

Unraveling every mystery and awakening
A understanding of His inspirations
His wisdom, joy, imagination—His way
Of freeing the soul from hatred and blame
Leaving only a trace of His elation to say
He has given the soul a new way, a new day
Breathed light into the darkness of worry
Blocked the obscurity that comes from pain
Birthed a love that is greater than fear
A love that is more alive than any dream

Alive, more brilliant than any sun
He only desires to free us from
The one who longs to destroy our soul
Leave us depleted, dead and alone
Without reason, hopeless and mournful
Filled with death and disillusionment

He frees our weary souls from this darkness
This fiend who reeks of destruction, despair
And reminds us why we should always be thankful
For the grace that gives our souls a way
To know the wonder of peace and praise
With faith to pray for the promise of love
That will cover every sin with His blood
And assure the soul that God above
Erases all doubt with assurance that He is
The satisfaction and salvation that comes
From trusting in His One and Only Son!

Faith

> And all things, whatsoever ye shall ask in prayer, believing, ye shall receive.
> —MATTHEW 21:22

Faith lifts the fear from my spirit
Lights the way toward a new day
Breathing hope into the moments
Softening my heart and soul as I pray
In words of praise, silence finds a way
To color my dreams in hues of soft gray
Reflections of kindness, mercy, grace

Faith brings me comfort when I'm feeling
Lost, alone, disillusioned—filled with fear
Dread that beckons to my dreams, my needs
Fantasies flavored with a bittersweet tear
Memories breathed through my every year
So brilliant, pure and wise—recollections so clear
They fade into the laughter, light and love

Faith haunts my heart in shadows so vibrant
Feelings so alive they dance across the soul
Whispering melodies, rich and warm echoes
Stained crimson from the heart to console
Songs of silent prayers, aware of the self-control
Lingering in the one who knows Him who will extol
Blessings from our heavenly Father, God of us all

Faith assures the mind that there will be time
To reach beyond the ashes of the unholy past
Discover the wonder of shimmering starlight
Filling the skies with blessings, so steadfast

They soar through the dreams who have outlasted
All the worries, sorrows and pain, the contrast
Of darkness and light, good and evil, hope and futility

Faith is the answer to our prayers, our desires
It feeds on the hope that it actually inspires
Reassures the soul of its place in heavenly realms
Thriving on love that builds up all the fires
Warming the spirit with peace that only requires
The knowing that God is alive amid angelic choirs
Singing to the soul of its home among the beloved

Faith reaches beyond our mind into our very core
Where we know that wisdom will assure a belief
That is living on the prayers and petitions we bring
To our Heavenly Father, the God who brings relief
He is the light, the insight, the One who comforts grief
He gave us this earth, even covering Adam with a fig leaf
He holds the heart in His palm, reassuring and calm

Faith this secure is faith that gives voice to every prayer
And faith this certain is faith God blesses beyond compare!

He is the wonder of my life

He is the wonder of my life
He heals my hurt, worry and strife
I long to give Him all of my doubt
Let Him use me and lift me out
From the disgrace I've been living in
The darkness that shadows me in sin
The hardness of a heart who knows
This Jesus will leave me smelling like a rose

He is the answer to all of my prayers
Without His love, my hopes would be in tears
He whispers kindness through my world
Mingling His joy with peace that He swirled
Into a mosaic of colors so brilliant and bold
It brought my heart to life and filled the mold
God had created when He made me long ago
Setting my spirit afire so that I am all aglow

He is the breath of grace falling over my soul
Sighing with a song of serenity that will console
Even the night runs away from the sweet light
That reflects from my touch as I continue to fight
For all that is good, all that He blesses, all His love
Tenderness and affection birthed from up above
On wings of sweetest faith, inspiring gentle grace
Which will leave me full of feelings I can't replace

Hallelujah sweet Jesus, the love of my lifetime
Hallelujah to the heavens where I will climb
As this world leaves me with one purpose, one goal
To glorify the Father, give Him devotion from my soul
Hallelujah sweet Jesus, the One I call my hope
The answer to my prayers, the reason I can cope
The music that feeds my spirit with kindness and love
The feeling that awakens when I look to heaven above

Pax vobiscum

Pax vobiscum—peace be with you

He came to earth, the perfect light
Faith, hope and love filled the night
He was more than merely the only way
He was the king of kings they often say

His love is wonder, joy and grace
He is the One who fills this place
With kindness beyond our dreams
Wisdom more alive than sunbeams

His laughter arrives with the rain
He relieves our sorrow and our pain
Delivers us from the sin in our past
In vibrant hues that leave a contrast

His glory arrives on the kiss of a tear
Shimmering so bright it melts the fear
Wipes away the silence with its insight
Whispers of elation like the moonlight

His life reminds that we hold this peace
From His spirit, . . . love will always increase
Because He came to give us a second chance
The miracle of a life alive with the romance

Peace be with you . . . is His wonderful vow
Filling hearts with inspiration to allow
His love to penetrate the center of a heart
With amazing blessings that will never depart

Enoch Walked with God

Enoch walked with God
Had faith beyond compare
With grace his heart was shod
He loved others in every prayer
His heart had a light they could share

In faith, he struggled through
Leading the way to God's joy and hope
He spoke of heaven and always knew
There was a grace to help him cope
His life was vibrating like a kaleidoscope

Enoch knew that God was his friend
He held onto the wonder of His presence
Felt His love wrap him up so to amend
Every worry, fear or anxiety—Omnipresence
Reminded him that life and love were God's presents

It was with great joy and a feeling of delight
That God brought him home—no death to divide
The Trinity held him up during his flight
Up, up, up to heavenly realms . . . the Bride
And, thanks to God, he hadn't even died

So walk on with God . . . let His light lead you
Through this old world, on into life everlasting
There isn't a doubt, His love will bring you through
Into the heart of paradise, where love is blasting
A feeling of joy, inspiration and knowing love is outlasting

A Hard Heart

A hardened heart
closed the mind, so unkind
left the soul without empathy
struggling to understand
the joy in Christ's gift to man
Salvation of the soul
a reason to hope, to grow
in the light, the love, the wonder
of a grace that made life kinder

A hardened heart
broke through the dreams
coloring everything
in seas of blackest sorrow
left the thoughts filled with despair
carried the fear to the soul
where it kept joy from rising up
and leaving a promise of Him who knows
that faith can brighten the darkness
with sincerity and assurance
that joy comes to the One who listens
to the prayers of true repentance

A hardened heart
gorged by lies from the deceiver
Jesus' adversary, the wicked one
who knows only to steal and destroy
love that flows into the light
from hearts who've learned to fight
the darkness, the hardness
with love that is gentle and kind
filled with faith that reminds
His light is inspired
His love is a burning fire

His grace is there for us
Salvation will always come
to those who pray from a heart
convicted by the Holy Spirit
who echoes His beauty in us!

> *Repent ye therefore, and be converted, that your sins may be blotted out, when the times of refreshing shall come from the presence of the Lord.*
> *—Acts 3:19*

Jesus, Use Me

Jesus, use me
so that I bring you glory
Jesus, use me
so that I bring light to the darkness
Jesus, use me
so that I bring hope to the hopeless

Use me for Your glory and honor
Use me for Your unending grace
Use me for Your brilliant worthiness
Use me for Your infinite wisdom
Use me for Your sparkling exaltation

Jesus, use me
so that I bring a calm to the storm
Jesus, use me
so that I make a right from a wrong
Jesus, use me
so that others see Your light in me

Use me for Your display of goodwill
Use me for Your heart's gentle care
Use me for Your honor and sanction
Use me for Your majesty and approval
Use me for Your name's praise and thanks

Jesus, use me
so that I bring faith to the spirit
Jesus, use me
so that I bring blessing to the weary
Jesus, use me
so that I bring love to the needy

Jesus, use me
so that I bring You to your people
Jesus, use me
so that I bring faith to the weak
Jesus, use me
so that I bring praise to your name

Jesus, use me
so that I bring a new journey
to the ones who follow after You
longing to reach their mission
on the path that is filled with your truth

Jesus, use me
so that I bring hope, faith and love
and every good thing that comes down
from the God who reigns up above

Take It to Jesus

There are things I take to the Lord
Little things—sometimes more
Important things, like pain and sorrow
Whispers of insight, melancholy
Darkness and dread, joy's caress
A longing, a hope, a dream of the best

There are memories, inklings, visions
Reminders of light that I might have left
Behind me, shimmering like sun or stars
Laughing to be praising Him with all their
Might, coloring the heart in hues of faith
Peace and inspiration, a song of pure grace

Some things are huge, bigger than I could say
Life changing thoughts—inspirational truths
Lingering promises that come from the spirit
Wisdom and strength caressing the naked feelings
With serenity and sensitivity, an abundance
Of breathless imaginings to brighten the world

There are reasons I can't possibly explain
That I pray for His love to penetrate like rain
Nourishing the laughter, the kindness, the praise
That is nurtured by this faith so alive it displays
A grace beyond picturing, a grace that is intense
Penetrating the very heart with its fervent gift

There are thoughts that I take to my Father
He always listens and continues to guide me
Through the shadows and doubts, the dread
That sometimes fills me with fear and brings
A tender tear . . . to haunt my soul with sorrows
Leave me wondering about what comes tomorrow

There are hues of inspirational wonders
Feelings that bless, thoughts to ponder
Gifts of prayer and faith that is aware
Our hearts and our souls are God's favors
Silencing our worries and filling us with
Creativity, brilliance, a muse so amazing

There are hearts that pour out hope
Souls that empty minds of all disquiet
Light up the darkness with imagination
Read through the poetry of the spirit
Dispelling all fear and awakening sincere
Appreciation of God who is our guide

There are reasons I can't possibly reveal
Truths to be told, answers that unfold
The warmth of a blessing, the gratitude
The gratefulness of a soul who knows
God is the answer—He is the only hope
He is the master of everything we know

God is the only One to cover us in love
Love so amazing it shines like the stars above
And reminds our spirits to fly like a dove!

There Are Days When I Just Can't Pray

There are days when I just can't pray
My heart and soul feel like they're so cold
I can't reach out, penetrate the darkness
With a light from my dreams, a feeling
A belief in the hope God brings when He
Caresses the thoughts with His kindness
Blessings that come from such enlightenment!

There are moments when I can't cry out
To the One who holds my dreams in His palm
The One who paints the rainbow in the sky
The One who always reminds me just why
I must reach beyond my pain and find a way
To appeal to Him with my faith, my prayer
For serenity and sincerity, a wisdom, a chance
To listen to His reply and hope with a heart
That believes and agrees—He is the only way
He is the confirmation of my heart's faith
He is the whisper of kindness when I pray
He is the answer to every problem I've known
The resolution to every worry I might have
The verdict to every misgiving in my plan

There are times when I can't be sure why
I have been given this life—this insight
This joy and peace—wisdom and grace
This feeling that believes in this God
Who brings me through the darkest storms
The deepest tragedies, the horrors
The risks and sorrows and discouragements
The shame and despair, all the troubles
Sometimes so unfair—living on a prayer
That I might not even be able to voice
But, my heart speaks the need, the plea

There are times when I just can't reveal
The need that fills my spirit with a prayer
It is a gentle petition, summoning the Lord
With all His light and love—His majesty
As praise fills up my soul and I know, above all,
That He is the One who knows my heart
And I only need the thought—to assure
He will hear my entreaty and answer me
With a loving confirmation that I will always be
His child, His friend, His miracle from heaven!

There are times when I can't even pray
But even then, I can find the way to say
God is my Father and I praise Him alway!

God Is Always Good

He was gone for all of that time
No one knew what his life was like
He could have been a thief or murderer
Only God knows all that he's done
Why would Daddy let him come back home?

He destroyed everyone's trust
He left here with half of Daddy's belongings
Where did he live while gone?
No doubt he was with drunkards and harlots
People who live in the darkest thoughts
With only doubt, fear and despair
He was living with the dreaded devils
His life was shadowed by his failures

He shouldn't have had the nerve to come back
Home, for him, should be off limits
He shouldn't be allowed to live here anymore

But Daddy killed the fatted calf for him
Gave him the best robe and his ring
Embraced him with a joy that only knows
He is the beloved son, his heart and soul
Why hasn't he ever killed a calf for me, though?

I asked Daddy why he was going to all this trouble
For a son who had only used and abused him
Given him nothing but worry and strife
Filled his mind with only regret, pain and trials
I asked him why, but Daddy only said . . .

**"Son, thou art ever with me, and all that I have is thine. It was meet that we should make merry, and be glad: for this thy brother was dead, and is alive again; and was lost, and is found."

So Daddy killed the fatted calf for my brother
My resentful, bitter heart was spurned
But I know my Daddy is filled with pure love
And He loves the prodigal with a spirit
That can only be described as merciful . . .
Compassionate and tolerant . . .
Much like the forgiveness that God sends
To the one who repents and believes
His grace is like a light shining through
The soul who knows His love is the treasure
That every prodigal seeks to accept

And, I, the son who was righteous yet resentful
Need his forgiveness just as much
As the roguish prodigal . . .

All I need to do is ask, and God's forgiveness
Will reach down and absolve me of my wrongs
I will ask and receive . . . because, like my Daddy..
God is always GOOD!

> And he said unto him, Son, thou art ever with me, and all that I have is thine. It was meet that we should make merry, and be glad: for this thy brother was dead, and is alive again; and was lost, and is found.
> —Luke 15:31–32

Believe

If you don't believe
It is for you, I grieve

If you don't see the truth
It could be you're a youth

If you don't understand His plan
Designed before the world began

If you don't take time to pray
There is still hope for God's way

If you don't trust His grace
His spirit, hearts will embrace

If you refuse to see God's glory
You may not appreciate His story

Please listen to His voice
You always have a choice

He is the way, the truth, the life
To save souls, He was the sacrifice

Simply listen to Him and *believe*
His Salvation you will surely receive

A Simple Faith

I'm no scholar
I don't know many things
I'm not so intelligent
That I can pass every test
I'm not a sage
A specialist or doctor
I don't research all the details
Or have great thoughts
My intellect isn't rewarded
With trophies or honors

I'm a simple woman
With humble beginnings
Modest ideas and unpretentious
Dreams . . . I am meek
Unsophisticated and unassuming
I'm uncomplicated, plain
And totally straightforward

But I know..
Beyond the shadow of a doubt
Jesus came to bring me
A way out of sin and immorality
He came to make a way
Where no way had ever been
He was nailed to a tree
Where He hung until death
Came to take Him away
Into the shadows of its grip
In three days, He arose
From the grave
Reminded us that He brings grace
A second chance, a new way
All we need to do is pray

For forgiveness and our sin
Will be pardoned
So we can speak with God
And He will answer
Our heart's yearnings

He will conquer
All our fears and tears
With His gentle love
That colors our whole world
In kindness, hope and joy
Faith that forever abides
On the heart, soul and mind
Where our love resides
And where His light abides
Stirring our feelings to delight
In the blessing of a heavenly Father
Who loves us with a love
That pierces the darkness
And lights up the heart
With peace that is alive
Dancing through the night
Freeing our soul with insight
Into the wonder of a faith
That believes His way of grace
Gives the wisdom to praise
The One who made a way
The One who we say
Is the answer to our prayers
The reason we have faith
The assurance of our salvation
Inspiration to always praise
The One who is our Savior!

He Is GOD

Every morning, as heaven sighs
There comes the dawning
Of hope inspired by the dreams
That beckon from hearts
Minds who breathe the light
Erasing the darkness of night

As a lemony sun rises to smile
On the gentle mountains
Across the green meadows
The hearts who whisper
Silent prayers, reflections
Grace so alive it ignites
Fires of praise, promises
Second chance to awaken
The soul to love unwavering
Love that we are savoring
With our dreams, our hope
The feelings that make us whole

Peace falls from the skies
Sighing like the fireflies
Who bless hearts with their light
Hovering over the prairies
So alive, dancing in the wind
Spinning tales of gentle faith
Making a way to the Creator's haven
Where there is only serenity
Faith that silences doubt and dread
Drinks in pools of liquid faith
Imagines the fanciful places
Only the heart can embrace
With its ability to pray
To the One who knows us better

Than any morning sun or rain
More than the whispers of wind
More than the gentle feelings
More than the lingering joy

Prayers of praise, praying
For God to know our hearts
Our thanks—the way we say
A prayer for Him to reach beyond
The thoughts and thinking
Into the heart and soul where we need Him
To see the Son rising fair
Upon the inspirations, the awareness
Of a light so big it outdoes the sun
It is a light from God's throne room
A light of pure, unconditional love!

A light that shines hope into the heart
A light that sparkles with pure joy
A light that twinkles with faith and promise
A light that never fades or expires
A light that glows beyond this world . . .
Into the universe where He is everything and more!

He is GOD!

Jesus Himself

The sweetness of a babbling brook
Whispering softly, gentle
Over smooth stones, nuggets
Rounded and curved
By so many years of running water
Tenderly caressing each rock
With a quiet dowsing of liquid
Thanks for the home
Nestled in the bend of woods
A forest of contentment
Peaceful and blessed
Like a prayer being spoken
In chattering acceptance
Of God's beautiful creation

The woodsy moment, in shadows
Breathless with affection
Graceful like the swirling waters
Warm like the morning,
Lemony sunlight piercing the skies
With heartfelt murmurs
Silent light shining with life
Expressions of hope, reflecting
The moments of wonder
Appealing to the heart and soul
In waves of kindness, roaring
Into the mind, soothing praise
In a voice of birdsong and winds
Erasing all the darkness
Pouring out faith into the core
Of the spirit's yearning
For more of God's restful vision
Alive in the one who knows Him
The way, the truth, the life

The answer to all pain and strife
The One who colors life
In hope and faith, love that is . . .

Jesus Himself

Arise from the mountains
Speak out from the shores
God, in all His mystery,
Arouses each heart to know
His captivating blessing
Mesmerizing the spirit
Sending out echoes of serenity
Into the heart who believes
He is the light of hope . . .
Arising like dawn, graceful
A peace that surpasses all
Understanding . . . it trembles
With its ability to give me . . . .

Jesus Himself

The reason I feel so very blessed
The reason I love from my depths
The reason I know He is with me
Living inside, guiding my spirit!

Our Greatest Need

She sits and listens
Intent on every word
Not once does she visit the kitchen
Where I need her help, her assistance
There is so much to do, so many tasks
And she simply won't help me

She sits at His feet
Listening and heeding
His every word brings a peace
To her expression . . .
What could He be saying?
She looks so content there at His feet
Smiling her love, so attentive

She should be helping me, shouldn't she?
I think I'll go in and tell Him . . .
Mary isn't helping me with the meal . . .
He'll surely make her come in and help me

When I told Him I needed her help with these things . . .

Jesus told me . . .

**"Martha, Martha, thou art careful and troubled about many things . . . but one thing is needful: and Mary hath chosen that good part, which shall not be taken away from her."

Yes, she sits at His feet, breathless with pleasure
She sees that this is what she needs . . .
His light poured out over her soul, shining in hope
Whispering love, coloring her thoughts
In brilliant rays of faith that comes to life with His words.

Just being with the Lord. This is our greatest need!

** Luke 10:41–42

In This Moment

Life goes by quickly
Time stands still for no one
It is through God's gift
Of life—that we can feel
The essence of hope
The wonder of faith
The beauty of grace
The whispers of peace
The sweetness of love

Life goes by so fast
We can't waste the moments
On darkness that tries
To take away our time here
With its dread and worry
Its heartaches and struggles

We know that it is time
To listen to the heart's light
Feel the joy inside our soul
The uplifting music of a heart
Who knows that God is alive
And He survives every test of time
To fill our lives with appreciation

Life moves so fast, like a beam of light
Never allowing us the time we want
But hurrying forward—on to tomorrow
The present moment lost to the past
And the day we've spent changed to history
Where we pull out its memory and charm
To reflect on the whisper of our heart

We know only the joy of this moment
The day will be gone before too long
We need to find the blessing already
Upon us, the beauty, the kindness, the love
That shines down like the morning sun
Caressing the life who is inspired by it all
The wonder of God's creation, His presence
His endless supply of gifts, His sweet blessing!

Never take for granted the love
That is poured out on souls from above!

Eternal Life

His love silences my fear
Relieves my pain, comforts my grief
His love reassures my spirit
Encourages my dreams, lights my heart
With a peace that never doubts

His love quiets all my tears
Eases my sorrow, helps me to breath
Deeply of the compassion, the kindness
That is His, my Savior, the One
Who gave me a second chance,
Saved me with His endless grace

His love calms all my worries
Soothes my dread and despair
Takes away the worst suffering
Reminds me to pray, to speak to Him
Believing that He will answer me
With a promise to always give hope
Courage that knows how to cope

His love urges my soul to listen
To the whisper of His kindness, His blessings
Poured out so that I only know
This peace that goes beyond description
So serene it feels like I am listening
To faith fulfilling all my wishes
Inspiring me to praise Him with my voice
In songs of thanksgiving because
He is worthy, He is worthy, He is worthy
He is the answer to my every need
The feeling that my heart believes
The wonder of a friend who I see
As the best friend I've ever had

The friend who brings life to my soul
The friend who is dancing in my heart
As He sings out His embrace, His touch
Bringing me to life with His sweet love

His love is the reason I know what it is
To believe in my soul that He will always be
Alive, surviving throughout time, to give each believer
The opportunity to feel His peace, His hope, His faith
The inspiration of a life that is knit from grace
The miracle of a love that brings us face to face
With a Savior who delivers from the darkest doom
Reassuring with His promise of a heavenly home

His love.. is my heart's greatest need
He is the answer to my prayer for peace
His love . . . is my music, my vision, my poetry
He is the light that shines down on me
His love . . . is the essential hope and I believe
He is the reason that I can worship in faith
His love . . . is my prayer, my solution, my key
To the wonder of a life sparkling with praise!

His love, my dear friend . . . dances and shines
Lighting my soul with His direction to eternal life!

His Light

Light, like the morning
Dawn's laughter
Reflecting so much joy
Sun silences the moon
Quiets the stars
Echoes brilliant hues
Of joy and insight

Light, like a whisper
Sunrise healing
Leftover darkness
Lingering fear, dread
Tears of regret
Pouring out peace
Threads of grace

Light, like a song
Rains down such hope
Never letting go
Of the wonder, the glow
Breathless as a caress
Embracing the soul
With a miracle

Light, like a prayer
Gentling the passion
Lingering, everlasting
Breaking through the thoughts
Clinging to the dream
Feelings who believe
In this undying appeal

Light, like a smile
Glowing in the heart
Baptizing thoughts
In purity, embracing
Melodies of grace
Bound up in praise
His wonder so amazing

Light, like a feeling
Pleading for healing
Breathless with desire
His passion is the fire
That welcomes faith
Unending conviction
Credence, alive

Light, like a promise
Resonating hope
In a single word, a vow
To always care, to spare
The soul its verdict
Lifting the spirit
To always know peace

Light, thriving on the spirit
Singing to the brilliance
Of a love so gentle
So fulfilling and willing
To bring His spirit to life
Vibrant on the inside
Of those who believe in Him

Light, like this
Blesses and believes
It is God, it is grace
Who frees the soul
From darkness that grows

Out of sin, faults
Forgiven by our one hope . . .

Jesus, Savior of the world!

Praising The King

The heart, the soul
Are all aglow
With love that rains down
Hope and joy
Peace and passion from above
Lighting the spirit
With sensitivity, fulfilling
Every thought, each dream
Beautiful grace
Sent on the wings of faith

The wonder of a love
Flowing through the veins
Inspiring such trust
Belief that awakens thanks
To the One who gives
His ultimate gift
The life that He lives
Dying on a tree
Inviting me to be free
Through His deliverance
From the darkest grief
He is the Savior
The One who makes a way
When all hope was lost
He always knew the cost
But still went to the cross

The miracle of His love
Fills hearts with assurance
He will always be available
Answering prayers
With His tender compassion
Pulling the lost

From the murkiest waters
Keeping them secure
In the arms of a harmony
So warm and pleasing
It feels like He has overcome
The loneliest night
The demons of fright
The dread of a plight
That seeks to destroy

His love is a gift
That gives unconditionally
With joy and faith
Abundant hope and grace
A light that never fades
With His still small voice
He gives us all a choice
And we can call upon His name
Whisper through faith
He relieves all pain
Paints the soul in hues
That glow with adoration
His love is forever stirring
Hearts to overflowing

I'm so thankful—eternally praising my King
He is my everything!

Dare to Believe

What courage she must have had
To believe in her heart
To shadow Naomi's steps
Follow her to another land
A place she'd never been

What courage she must have felt
To walk the path toward a place
She'd never seen herself
But had only heard and dreamed about
A land faraway from her people
A land where she believed
God would bless her completely

What courage she must have known
To have gleaned from the crops
Of a stranger to her own soul, a stranger
Who would offer her His land to glean
All the food she could gather
More than she would have expected

What courage she must have borne
To have proposed to love someone
She had only known for a short time
Someone who might or might not
Extend a welcome to her proposition
Would he be pleased with her?
Or would he downright reject her?

It would be only a short while
Before Boaz became her spouse
The one who would father the child
Who would make her the great grandmother
Of King David . . . a man after God's own heart

Who would also be the forefather of One,
The light of the world, Jesus Christ

What courage she must have known
To become grandparent to God's only Son!

> But now thy kingdom shall not continue: the Lord hath sought him a man after his own heart, and the Lord hath commanded him to be captain over his people, because thou hast not kept that which the Lord commanded thee.
> —1 Samuel 13:14

Some Days

There are days when I don't feel
Like listening to God's will
There are days when I don't know
What it is to truly hope
There are days when I just can't say
Prayers that leave me feeling blessed
As if the Lord has poured out His love
Rained down His joy, His light, His glory
Onto my soul, into my spirit, revealing
The wisdom of listening, hearing
All of the love that He is giving
Love like this is love that is fulfilling

There are days when I don't understand
What it is to live in God's plan
There are days when I don't imagine
I'll ever make it to the promised land
There are days when I just can't say
What I feel in my heart, the best part
Of being a child of the King, a child
Who is living to give back to Him

There are days when I don't appreciate
The blessings He gives me, the kindness
The endless feelings of a grace
That fill my heart with complete faith
There are days when I wish I could say
I know where I'm going with this life
I know what it means to conquer strife
I know all about this eternal grace

But. I am merely a simple woman
With only my bible and my hope
My belief in the One who came to earth

To die on a tree knowing I'd believe
He came back to life, resurrected
A risen Savior who I can always know
Will light up the darkness with His love
Answer my prayers with His resolutions
Fulfill my heart's needs with His promises

Yes, there are days when I can't answer
I don't know the when, the why or the where
I don't know how or who.. I only know, for sure,
That Jesus is the answer to every problem
He provides the comfort through the storms
And leaves me feeling certain that I am loved

There are days when I just can't pray
But there are endless ways I can say
He holds the key to my heart and soul
Without Him, I wouldn't be whole
I'm so very thankful He is the anchor
I will always hold onto Him and know
He will make a way where no way was before
He will light the darkest dread with faith
And He will silence every thought of doubt

I love Him more today than I ever have

God's Muse

Light pours through branches
Caressing the earth
With a kindness so rare
So gentle, warm
It feels like hope coloring
The heart in vibrant
Layers of laughter and love

There are shadows of oaks
Birch, locust and pine
Reflections of the earth
Calling to the sun
Silent screams for peace
Baptizing every whisper
In songs of praise

Rainbow yearnings
Fall among the seas
Promising their blessing
Their waves of dreams
To caress the thoughts
With prayers, hope
Sincerity that calms the wind

Showers of dripping liquid
Cool and comforting
Restoring the heart's stillness
With music from beads
Falling in streams
Restoring the beauty
To a clean, clear fantasy

Where hope meets fate
There breathes a gentle grace
Truth calling from heaven
Reminding hearts to worship
The One who created it all
The sun, the moon and the stars

All the beauty of God's muse

Life's Echo in Hell

Eternal, alive like the sun
Caressing dreams
With whispers of hope
The silence of abundant promise
Raining down showers, songs
Grace penetrating the ones
Who know immortality
Unending love, breathed out
From the caress of cool,
Clear waters roaring, liquid
Pools of inspiration, soothing
Calming aching spirits
Those who grieve for the death
Which can never come
As the soul wishes to disappear
Undone by the echoes
Shadows of a love gone, long gone

In solitude, silence sighs
Deepening the desire
For a end to the dream
Fading into the shadows
Wishing, wistfully,
For the time when this
Brooding flower
Love lost, so long now
Faded into the secret
Place of death, decay
Demise so real it never fades
Yet, eternally, in undying
Unforgettable memory
There is the echo of its yearning
Singing into awaiting ears

We will on, forever,
Even though the love of life
Has been gone for so long
Dead yet never dying
Always screaming in silence
Lingering on the solitude
Singing to the soul in blue
Worn, dull and pale
Diminished by the thoughts
Which dread immortality
Life's echo in hell

Eternally Grateful

Wildflowers hesitate,
Breathing in the clear air
Inspiration so brilliant, alive
With whispers of faith
Purity in gulps of gasping, panting
Flavors of chasteness
Wholesomeness . . .
Transparent feelings, blessed
Healing all the past . . .
With clean, cool innocence

In the meadows,
Over the mountains,
Tiny petals emerge, soft
Tender reflections
Of the earth's heartfelt
Laughter, its peace
Serenity so blessed, so honest
It feels like a smile
Falling down from the heavens
Exalting the One who created
Every petal, each stem
All the laughter from Him
Poured out on an earth
Too lonely, too timid
To know a God this big
God who is like a gentle embrace
Yet, fills up the whole place
With His love, His stirring, His spirit
His grace and sacredness

In the dreams,
Coloring the reflections
In gaping grape and soft rays

Of tangerine sunrises
Pink skies on the horizon
Where mystery smiles questions
Through the impressions
Stifling a sigh, a sign
That life has just begun
For the one who believes
He sees the rising Son as the
Caress of a hand so big
So wise and kind and sure
That He is like light
Raining hope from the skies
Painting hearts in faith
Baptizing souls in amazing peace
He is the silence and the shout
And He never leaves anyone out
Of the song He sings,
The song of redemption
Faith's melody sparkling through
The night sky like pearls
Glimmering in the heavens
Reaching down to remind
He is alive and He shines into
The one who listens to His
Direction, His way is prayer
Praise and worship so sacred
It affects every pore,
Each sweating drop, echoing
His wisdom, His love
That knows only generosity

Skies soften who know
He comforts, heals and radiates
The meaning of grace, peace
Love that is so alive
It feels like the trembling
Thunders, the caress

Of rain, soft and flowing
Down to touch the spirit
With aliveness that thrives
On giving, filling hearts
With gentle breaths . . .
Love so radiant it lights
Up the entire world
With His glory, His splendor
Magnificence so praiseworthy

Praise Him . . .
Eternally, wholly
Forever and ever!

Praise Him

Praise Him
With my thoughts
Tender, heartfelt reflections
Ideas that create peace,
A melody of affections . . .

Praise Him
With my dreams
Kind and sweet regards
Toward the One I believe
Created and gave to me . . .
a life filled with purest love

Praise Him
With my hopes
For all the joy life brings
With light of laughter,
Smiles so free and satisfying

Praise Him
With my faith
Believing that He is light
Shining through my heart
Reflecting all my compassion
In music of the everlasting

Praise Him
With my sincerity
Promising to give generously
The parts of me who imagine
Grace beyond my reveries
Mercy that brings certainty
That His love is the way for me
To know what it means to be

Delivered from sin, saved, redeemed
By a Savior who has blessed me with . . .

Love that is forever in my favor!

What Love Isn't

Love isn't about
The many times you cried
It is about the moments
When you smiled and laughed
With joy that poured out light
Into your heart and soul

Love isn't about
The many times you failed
It is about that one day
When everything felt just right
And all your heart was alive
With the music of a tender delight

Love isn't about
The many times you doubted
It is about that special faith
You had in the one you loved
The one who taught you that hope
Comes from giving of your trust

Love isn't about
The many times you worried
It is about that certainty
Inspiring your soul to dream
And believe in the acceptance
Of a heart who keeps on wishing

Love isn't about
The times it let you down
It is about the times when it lifted you up
Breathed peace through your heart

Colored your life in a promise of affection
Elation from knowing God has surely blessed you . . . .

With Love

You Are ALIVE!

You smile down
Your lemony dawn
Whispering joy
Through my thoughts
Inspiring my heart
To listen to the grace
Pouring over me
With a song of praise

You laugh through the skies
Brightening my life
With music that never fades
It's sweet and awakens
My soul to the radiance
Of silent sighs
Reassurance, breathtaking
Serenity, so soothing
So captivating

You gentle even the wind
With your kindness
Your mercy and peace
The way You have, so generous
With love that is healing
Stirring the soul to believe
Coloring the life
In soft swirls of appreciation
Sense of admiration

You baptize my spirit
In faith that comforts, uplifts
Guides me through
All the worry and fear
Pain, struggles and tears

Encouraging me to keep dreaming
Keep believing in my dreams
And listening to the Holy Spirit
Who dwells inside of me
Breathing hope into my yearnings
Sighs so calm, so consoling
I know the love that You give
Is a love that will forever live

You are the One
Who makes my life complete
You light the heart and soul
With love that is devoted
To giving, fulfilling, revealing
All the wonder of Your gifts
The kindness that sustains
The beauty in everything

Your love is like a star shining
Down into the thoughts
Coloring the mind in hope
Forbidding the heart to pine
Leaving only the glow
An extraordinary love
Burning through the dark
Stealing the hearts
Who know that You are alive
You are mightier than time
Your light will forever be mine

Thank You, dear God
For Your light, Your love
Your inspiration and encouragement
You are wise, insightful, compassionate
And, I fully love YOU!

Lead Me On

When fear tugs at my dreams
Shadowing the joy
With dread and dismay
Discouraging the light with dark
That echoes alarm
Through the silhouettes
Of anguish and pain . . .

I turn to the One who brings me
Through the storms
Across the mountains of melancholy
The gloom that explodes
With its roaring rage, its angry
Rays of restraint, dampening
The faith that leads me to His grace
Where I can find a way
Through the worry, the ache

I turn to the One to whom I pray
Thy will be done—knowing
His way brings the light to my heart
The hope to my thoughts
The peace to my turbulence

Thy will be done is the way to say
He is the only One who remains
When all hope has gone and the pain
Lingers on my heart, overpowering
The wonder of a love so alive
It is like a raging fire inside
Dancing through the murk and mire

When all hope has gone and I'm alone
With the anxiety, tempting
Me to listen to its panic as it trembles
Through my heart, through my thoughts
Beckoning for me to a place, so anxious
Filled with fears, tears and years
Of misunderstood feelings and doubt
Pouring over my heart's quest
For a peace that only grace can harvest
With its phenomenal mercy, its prayer
For His hand to fall over my soul
With a love that is vibrant and bold
A love that only God himself can show
To the spirit who believes and receives
The Son, the answer to every fear
The comfort for every doubt
The healing from the inside out

Thy will be done is the prayer I pray
When I need to say, "Dear God . . .
Take away this pain, this sorrow, and
Fill my heart with a love only You
Can inspire and assure, bring to life
Inside my soul where You remind me . . .
Courage in life comes from Your direction
The knowing that bravery is a sign
That You are the Lord of my spirit!"

To Him I Will Cling

As I go through this life
With all its pain and strife
I reach out toward the hand
Who offers the promised land
In Him, I find my true peace
Through love that will not cease
He assures my heart of His grace
Comforts my fears with His embrace

As I meet with struggles and labor
He reminds me to love my neighbor
With a love that He inspired within
When He forgave all of my sin
His light glows through the heart
With a radiance only He can impart
He reflects all the hope and belief
Showing me where I can find relief

As I reach toward the rising Son
With a hope for every loved one
I feel Him raining down joy inside
In Him, I know I can always confide
His wonder fills my life with hope
Assuring my soul that I can cope
He whispers through my every prayer
Promising that He will always be there

As I smile into the face of my Savior
Who kindly forgives my misbehavior
I know that I've discovered the solution
To all my pain, sorrow and persecution
He is the breath of joy and insight
He inspires my heart to delight
In the love that only He can bring
To His hand I will forever cling!

In Her Garden

Her eyes begin to sparkle
With joy from within
Pleasure only found from
Sharing the heart with a friend
Elation only known with
The whisper of intimacy baptized
In laughter, smiles, euphoria
Left on the heart who listens
Silently, to the roar of solitary
Gratification taken from the spirit
Who knows the sweetest blessings,
The greatest gift from God's
Genius, His expressions of care.

Her wonder is alive on her grin
As she digs, plants and weeds
Clearing away debris from the past
Renewing the deep, dark earth
With fresh mulch and bits of protection
From the frost that still could pour over
The lives who have only just begun
As Spring light flavors the dirt
In rich, nutritious sunshine

Her heart is betrayed by the delicate
Growth, the bulbs poking their heads
Through the earth, reminding us all
That the life of the garden is nearly
Ready to spring into this season
With heady, fragrant gifts from
Our Creator, the One who knows us
The way the seasons know the plants
And rain down hope, faith and peace
Through the spiritual light lingering

On prayers and praise poured out from
Those who know the amazing, tantalizing
Charm of the tulips, daffodils and roses
The lupine, the delphinium and dahlia
The luscious love from a quiet, smooth
Poppy, a marigold, a lily or a pansy
All the ones who drench the earth
In persuasive blooms, delicately planned
To color the world in vibrant designs

Her spirit is soaring like the cardinal
Alive with the moments of preparation
Forming cool, dark holes for roots
To awaken to, dig into, forage for
The nourishment that will always bring
Peace like rain falling softly, soothing
Healing the mind of all its anxieties
Sighing like the winds through the branches
Of oak, birch and emerald pine trees
Laurels alive with arising ferns
Exhaling psalms that emerge from the
Caress of God's breath falling gently
Over the garden where she dances
With flowers who only know her as
The grower, the one with the power
To make even the wildflowers bend
To her will, to her gift for gardening
With a love that is inspired by Him
Giver of the sunshine and the rainfall!

Beneath Her Tears

Tears pooled at the edge of
Brilliant blue, intelligent eyes
Her heart poured out her feelings
The dread, the darkness
The desperation of a situation
That was covered in anxiety
A place of fear and dismay,
Shadowed by worry and despair

Her eyes met mine before her gaze fell
It was apparent that she felt alone
Without a friend—anyone to speak up
Remind the world that she was someone
She wasn't just another addict, hooked
By the sensations of hope that relieved her
If only briefly, from the loneliness
The aching isolation that was only worse
Because she was addicted to a feeling

She stooped, obviously sensing the rejection
That fell all around her, discouraging her
Darkening her thoughts and her dreams
Echoing the dread that had filled her life
Since she was young, before she'd even known
What it meant to be an addict, someone
With a habit that led to a compulsion
An obsession with a pill so potent, so powerful
It flooded every thought with the craving

Silence screamed into the shadows of her space
Where she knew only the seclusion that told her
If she met someone else's gaze here, in church,
She would only meet with a judgement, a verdict
Sentencing her to the assurance that even here
Among the believers, she'd only find condemnation

Her heart almost stopped when she met my eyes again
And I smiled quickly, before she had the chance to look away
I was startled by the beautiful smile that came to life
In this face so barren of hope, so filled with loss
With a smile, I found the opening to let my light shine
Sharing with this broken soul a part of the spirit
That told me Jesus himself would wipe those tears away
With love that will always mean He is alive, aware
He is the answer to every prayer, each need, all things
Are blessed by the One who shines His light
Through you and me, His followers, His people

Today, she is shining His light upon so many souls
Those who needed her smile and her spirit
To sing praises for His amazing grace and peace
His wonderous way of mending the heartbreak

Happy Easter Day

This is the day
When we reach toward heaven
Whispering, praying
To the Creator of everything
The One who gave us
A second chance to say to Him
Thank you, God . . . for grace
Thank you for this chance
To reach out in faith
And take the hand that was nailed
To a cross just three days before this.

This is the day
When we yearn to lift our voices in praise
Of the One who made a way
For us to finally say
We can visit heaven someday
Even though we've sinned along the way
He didn't leave us in our sin
But chose to save us from anguish

This is the day
When we whisper through our tears
Joy that is beyond words
Because we have access to the One
Who made a way for us to go home
A way for us to pray and praise
A way for us to know the meaning of grace

This is the day
When faith will find a way
To finally reach heaven and say
He is risen—He is alive!
He survives the tests of demise

He is the Savior—He is the life
He is ascended to heaven
Where He awaits His many disciples
Those of us who know Him
As Jesus Christ, the victor
The way to finally find true life
Hidden inside the soul
Where He left us the Holy Ghost
To remind us that He abides
There, inside, ALIVE . . .
Providing a light to shine
Brighter than moon and stars
Wiser than the lemon sun
Purer than the hope of a love
This beautiful, this kind
This full of everlasting life

This is the day
When I come to God to say
Thank you—I praise You
For this Easter, I remember
Your love, Your joy, Your grace
The home where you made a place
For me to come into your embrace
Hallelujah—Happy Easter Day!

Sonshine

Breathing hope
Into my heart and soul
He always knows
Just what I'm in need of
He always assures
That His grace is ever present
A constant source of strength
A power freeing me from sin
A kindness so much a part of Him

Breathing faith
Into my spirit's core
He frees me from the darkness
Faded into shadows of disease
He silences the screams
Of loneliness and grief, promising
Relief from all the dread
The feelings that leave me
Angry, isolated and depressed

Breathing love
Into the center of my soul
He declares to me that His love
Will awaken the praise I know
Calls out to my heart to honor
The One who gave up His life
So that I could live without strife
So that I could know real delight

When I ignore
This joy that He pours
Into my spirit
With His gentle peace
I feel like I have betrayed

The One who makes my life
A place of hope, faith and love
A place where He is the One
To shine like the soul's Son!

> *And now abideth faith, hope, charity, these three; but the greatest of these is charity.*
> *—1 Corinthians 13:13*

Good Friday

Beaten beyond recognition
Tortured in ways we'd like to ignore
Because our hearts are disturbed
By the darkness that fell across our world
When Jesus was dying on a cross,
Crucified for the sins that were ours
But were also sins we'd never pay for
Because He gave up His life at Calvary
Where we could visit and find redemption
Forgiveness for those sins we committed
Pardon for the crimes of our spirits

Barely breathing, He spoke the words . . .
"It is finished" before leaving this world
For the hereafter, where we were so sure
We'd never be able to talk with Him again
Or feel the wonder of His kindness,
His gentleness or sensitivity, His wisdom
Or His grace and penetrating compassion

Someone offered Him their tomb
A rich man, who believed in His love
Others were willing to clean Him up
Placing His body where no one could harm
The One who was loved beyond words
The One who was at the heart of hope
The One who made us feel so sure
God would have His way—His day
Filling lives with assurance of His grace

He left this world and went to the tomb
Wrapped in grave clothes and spices
Placed in the heart of the earth
Where we were sure His body would be

Secure until we could sleep in peace
Sleep away the grief that was ours, complete
In a way that only reminded the heart
Of His death, His departing from the lives
Who loved Him more than anything else

As His lifeless body lay in that tomb
Hearts grieved for the One who had come
To bring love to the dark and lonely world
To shine a light into the lives who knew
Only the dimness of despair and depression

With Him, life had finally been better
Now, with Him gone, hearts were mourning
With a solemnity that was so very painful

That was the day that they lay God to rest
That was the day that love was placed to the test
That was the day that our lives were blessed!

> When Christ hung, and bled, and died, it was God saying to the world, *"I love you."*
> —Billy Graham

Wilderness Prayers

Nature breathes peace through the whisper of leaves, the tenderness of a silent breeze, the roar of thunder and even the rain's sincerity. Nature breathes harmony.

—BY POET

Let me tell you a story . . . about a land of hope
There, on the shores of promises,
Standing taller than tall—the way to cope
Rustling leaves fall at her feet,
Whispering away the chill, calm air
Autumn singing through the leaves, blending
Colors of boldest crimson and tangerine
Gold so brilliant it lingers on the heart
Encouraging the blessings that are so alive
During the harvest, when souls are spellbound
By heavenly halos of buttered corn, apples
And the sing song dances of branches
Awaiting the final leaf's falling to the ground

Yes, winter will come and with it
The silence of fresh fallen snows and memories
Haunting the spirit with tender breaths
Clinging to the sharp pores of this impression
Where crisp chilly air seems to beckon
The heart outdoors, into the unsoiled world
A winter wonderland, so alive and so perfectly
Breathtaking in every way, with every prayer

Spring unlocks the treasures of God's paintbrush
With vibrant hues of golden-haired petals
And lively, lush scarlet, purple and lavender
All the colors so vivid and dramatic, like a shout

To the heart—ringing with melodies so enchanting
Magnificent thoughts rush to the surface
A mind hypnotized by nature, the miracles, the feeling
Inside those who know that nature is God's great blessing
To all the spirits who long for His heaven on earth

Forever and Always

Beneath the spell
Of stars, moon and night
Breathing the peace
The hope which I write
Soft hues of life
Moments to surprise, excite

Under the influence
Of dancing dreams, enchanting
Grace so abundant and wise
Beauty and love it is planting
Laughing in tender blessings
Faith is a light God is granting

Beneath the charm
Of hearts filled with love
Wonders so vibrant
Alive with joy from above
Sincere as His Son
Who brings peace like a dove

Under the power
Of beauty unbelievable
Splendor so alive
The soul is inconceivable
Kindness whispers
A song that is achievable

Beneath the allure
Of glorious prayer and praise
Comes a feeling, a sense
Of elation that will amaze
The heart who knows
His love is forever and always

Blessings

Send down Your blessings, dear Lord
Allow me to feel Your kindness and love
The mercy that comes from Your Son
Grace so alive it feels like I've broken free
Of the sins, the flaws, the darkness
That penetrates my spirit with pain, anger
And all of the things that I wish to leave
Behind me, in the past where I used to be

Send down Your blessings, dear Father
Cause me to know You better with each miracle
Blessings of love so warm I feel the affection
Tenderness like a hope that colors the heart
In hues of insight and delight, beauty so wise
It pours out joy and peace, feelings that believe
Only the Son and His grace can free the soul
From the distress that brings doubt and depression
Dread that beckons hearts to feel the anguish
Of knowing that trouble is always there, haunting
With its never-ending grief, its pang of misery

Send down Your blessings, dear God
Remind me that You are there, alive
Willing to give me a second chance, a new life
Born out of the love that Jesus taught us to know
With His grace and His wonder, His courage
All the songs of a heart who gives unconditionally
With a purity, a promise that is more sure
Than the love that falls all over with its truth
When we are brought to our knees
At the foot of the cross where we can see
Love that brings true peace, true belief

Truth that sounds like strength and relief
Love that is alive in the soul who believes

Jesus is the answer to every prayer we breath

Freedom in Christ

Silent, He bore His cross
Endured the pain and shame
Under the scrutiny
Of scoffers filled with sin
Feeling their mutiny

Silent, He bore His Cross
Gave up His life for those
Who left Him suspended
Between heaven and earth
Alone, undefended

Silent, He bore His cross
Erasing our sin debt
Knowing He gave His all
Reminds us what was paid
So on God we can call

Silent, He bore His cross
In three days, on Easter
Jesus Christ rose again
Alive, He came to give
Freedom to souls, A M E N!!!

The Best Blessing

God sends miracles
In the form of blessings
Little things and big things
Some life changing
Others merely affecting
The heart's smile

God sends marvels
To the hearts and souls
Who listen for His love
To pour out across the soul
Who knows that He is there
Alive inside each prayer

God sends wonders
To guide the gentle spirit
One who knows that
His love is forever with us
Guiding toward the victory
Of a heart who believes

God sends His blessings
To hearts and souls who need
To feel His presence, His spirit
In hues of tender affection
Brought to life in the heart
Who knows *He is the best blessing*

Baptized into Hope

Staring up to the night sky
Stars and moon, clouds passing by
Dancing alive, caress of lights
Gentle as the hope that comes to life
When I see this breathtaking display
Laughing and smiling like they are praising
The Creator of them all, the One
Who lights up the moon and the sun
With His inspirations of peace and hope
His amazing wonders of grace
Pouring out love through the heart
Who welcomes His presence with faith
That He is the greatest blessing
More sacred than space so alive
It seems like a prayer from the night
Falling through the silence, breaking
Every thought with a sense of peace
That fades into the shadows,
Hues of sapphire dreams and halos
Of angel wings reminding the soul
To always know that the Creator
Not the creation—should be praised
By you and me—His creations

He is the maker of everything
He is the flame within the fire
He is the light that guides the night
He is the journey of spring to winter
He is the joy that makes real laughter
He is the One who I worship
And He is the One who gives my life purpose

He is the meaning of my yearning
He fills all my heart with assurance
That He is alive and because He lives
I will survive all that comes to me
Sorrow, grief, pain, depression and despair
Because of His love I can be certain
I will make it through this world
Secure in the Father's love, sure
That I know the love that came down
To die on a cross so we wouldn't need to

Because of this Love that brings hope
I can live justified by the cross
And saved by the resurrection of One
Who made me and gave me
Salvation, Redemption, Deliverance
I am so grateful for my Savior above!

I'll Follow Him

There is a love that is like no other
Love so alive it colors the life
In light, in fire, in the music of smiles
It is wise, beautiful and warm
Filled with such wonder, like the Son
Who knows that we are His gifts
From a Father who is pure love

There is hope that is vibrant and strong
Hope that is untainted by worry or strife
It is like laughter, lingering in delight
It fills the heart with kindness, inspiring
Splendor beyond dreams, loveliness
That the Lord brings with His grace

There is faith that is genuine, authentic
Faith that sings of wisdom and understanding
It fills the mind with insight into the soul
Knows the meaning of mercy, blessing and prayer
It baptizes the soul in joy that always knows
He is alive, a light, a fire blazing in the heart
Who knows that His faith rages out of control

There is the One who makes a way for us
Where no way has been known,
On the path that leads to life with Him
In a heavenly home . . .

Listen to the heart who reveals Jesus to the soul
There you will find a love that only God can bestow

Fear of the Lord

The enemy tries to destroy lives
He thrives on darkness, dread and death
He likes to tell the spirit lies
He whispers fear into the depths of men
Taking away their faith in God's plan

When one repents and believes in Him
Who was sent into the world
To bring the soul salvation from hell
And give us hope of a heaven above
Where there will be unconditional love –
The fear of death is less powerful

The fear we felt when under conviction
Fear that reminded us we need a Savior
One who will redeem our heart and soul
From the sin we need deliverance from . . .
Is a fear that should be no more
Once we've been introduced to the Savior
The One who made a way for us
At the foot of the cross, there is salvation

The fear of the Lord, a reverential fear
Is such a wise feeling, a fear
That reminds us we are small, a child in His sight
And He can, like any good Father,
Chastise us for our sin—even though
We don't always understand

Fear is the devil's tool to fool us
Into believing we're not the children of God
Never allow your heart to fall under
The spell of the enemy who would like you to believe
You aren't really saved,—you're still going to hell

Know that our Father,
Who is deserving of our reverent fear,
Will never leave us nor forsake us
We can never be plucked from His grasp
Even though He may chastise us for sin
He will never let us fall into hell
Where the devil hopes to obscure our faith
Beneath the darkness of his hatred

We are children of the living God
And He is abiding inside our hearts
Never let the devil put fear inside you
That produces a fear that should have been
Put behind you when you were saved
By the gift of grace poured out on us
Who place our faith in God's Son, Jesus Christ

And I give unto them eternal life; and they shall never perish, neither shall any man pluck them out of my hand.
—John 10:28

Loving God

How do I love God . . . I wonder silently
Do I send Him prayers
Praise Him with all my dreams
Do I love Him with my laughter
With my poetry
Do I love Him with my soul
When I listen to His scriptures

How do I love God . . . I wonder to myself
Do I whisper my adoration
On the hymns I sing
Do I breathe praise into my wishes
For His light to embrace me
Do I linger in the hues of His creativity
His creation

How do I love God . . . with all of my heart
Do I simply feel His blessings
Poured out upon my soul
Do I know His love—without conditions
Capturing my heart
With love that is so tender
It feels like stardust sparkling
Inspiration into my spirit

How do I love God . . . I welcome Him within
Where His Holy Spirit reflects the sweetness
Of grace so vibrant and soothing
Love so alive and moving
The light of joy that brings me truth . . .

I love Him with my spirit
I love Him with my thoughts
I love Him with my kindness
I love Him with my heart

How do I love God?
I love Him with my all!

The Comforter

He is interested in more than
The enormous happenings
Like worries and wars, weakness'
Darkness that shadows
Even the most beautiful thoughts

He cares about the little things
The flowers, the moon and the stars
The sunlight flickering through the trees
The mountains, the seasons, the winds
The joy that comes from His gentleness

He listens to the smallest prayer
For a promise that lives to become
A actuality as wonderous as a dream
A truth that survives every dread
A breath of hope within the spirit

He stirs up the inspiration and wishes
Of a heart who is alive with sensitivity
Magnificent faith that falls on souls
Who know that His love is eternally
Blessing everyone who truly believes

He shares His Holy Spirit with the one
Who knows that He lives inside, abiding
On the heart who feels so close to Him
Accepts the love He gives with praise
That comes from the spirit of sweet grace

He leaves the mind questioning His embrace
The love that comes from a tender gift
Comfort so soothing it feels like a chance
To reach beyond the world into the heavens
Where He shines His light always and forever

He sends down His love to those who know Him
And feel His presence with them in every prayer
Through every scripture reading, each devotion
He lingers on the thought of one who knows He is
Alive within the heart and soul, always so earnest

He will never leave the heart who knows His love
Is the one thing that makes life seem so good
It is the hunger for His kindness that stirs fires
Of passionate yearnings—desire for His miracles
Brought to life inside the soul who sincerely believes

He listens to the big prayers and the small prayers
He never turns a deaf ear to those who are heartfelt
Prayers that lift the spirit with generosity and altruism
The thoughtfulness of those who love without conditions
Because they listen to the One who hears the prayers they send Him!

>*I will not leave you comfortless: I will come to you.*
>—John 14:18

Prayer Warrior

Prayers plunge, faithful to believe, from souls
Hope longs to know His guiding light, His love
Kindness felt on those who God's love controls

Shining gentle like stars and moon above
Brilliant breaths of a song dancing freely
Hope longs to know His guiding light, His love

Whispers of His light fall soft, ideally
Breaking through the hearts who are hard and dark
Brilliant breaths of a song dancing freely

Laughing through the worry and fear, a spark
Abiding inside the one who knows grace
Breaking through the hearts who are hard and dark

Yearnings flow from spirits who do embrace
His never ending joy, inspiring thanks
Abiding inside the one who knows grace

Effective prayer silences life's blanks
Prayers plunge, faithful to believe, from souls
His never ending joy, inspiring thanks
Kindness felt on those who God's love controls

I Am the Clay

Hands move hastily, yet gentle
Perfecting the design
With creative fingers, sensitive
To the clay, the substance
That will be brought to life
With the subtle hints of wonder

Hands shift clay into pieces
Of earthen vessels, vibrant pottery
Terra cotta turned into graceful
Jugs. Pitchers and bowls
Delicious works from strokes
Both tender and persuasive

Hands change clay from soft
Supple mud to delicate formations
Brought to life by enchanting
Hearts who give their best to craft
Out containers worthy of the word
Perfection, flawless, whole, finished

Like God above who works with us
Creating something wonderful,
Something complete and whole
Because He gives the very best
To those He ingeniously changes
From dirty mud to miraculous creations

> *O house of Israel, cannot I do with you as the potter? saith the Lord. Behold, as the clay is in the potter's hand, so are ye in mine hand, O house of Israel.*
> —Jeremiah 18:6

Everlasting Love

Love like this is my inspiration
It brings pure grace to my spirit
Sings of a joy that is beyond words
Breathes a prayer from my soul
Leaves me with a light which reflects
Only the peace that comes about
When Jesus abides inside a heart

Love this wise is my life's guide
Through darkness, tears and fears
Across feelings of dread and despair
Around storms that fill me with doubt
Beyond the nightmares of the past
Amidst the whispers of resentment
During the worst that comes to haunt

Love this strong uplifts my hope
Calms my worries and anxiety
Assures me that I can do what I need to
Supports me with a melody so beautiful
Cheers my heart with incredible thanks
Bolsters all my dreams so they grow
Comforts me through pain and strife

Love this alive is my soul's vibrant star
The feeling poured out through my life
Expressing the joy, peace, insight
Wonders of precious smiles inviting bliss
Warmth that comes from giving praise
Sacred prayers that come to life
Stirring hearts to give their best

Love like this is God's gift of grace
The way toward hope that is forever
Kindness that brings true freedom
Salvation from the One who created . . .
Every heart, each soul, everyone—
Who has a hunger for His presence
To become reality, genuine redemption

This is the love that saved me
This is the love that gave to me
The most amazing grace, true faith
In the Son of God, my Savior –
Jesus Christ, the answer who came
To give us everlasting life!

God's Child

As a child of God
The One who brings me
Through the darkest dread
Through the fears that taunt me
Through the tears that haunt me
Through all the worry, pain and doubt
Through the shadows of regret

As a child of God
The God who gives me grace
Answers my prayers of faith
Assures me that there is a way
Even though my mind can't accept

As a child of God
The One who lights up the night
With moon, stars and dreams
And lights up the day with rays
Of sunshine laughing in hues
Of lemony joy and butter like hope

As a child of God
The God who makes a way
Where no way has been before
The God who brings me a second chance
When I've made the worst mistake
The God who lives to be the answer
To all my prayers, petitions and pleas

As a child of God, the living God . . . .
The One who is my answer to every worry
The One who shares His love and spirit with me
The One who I believe in—with all my faith

This is the God I want to praise
With all my heart and soul
With everything within my control
With all my words and deeds
With everything I believe

This is the God who is everything to me!

On the Inside

The hope that comes alive
On the inside
When I allow God to smile
Through my life
Forever alive, a light
Shining bright, glimmering
On the inside . . .

The faith that sings of thanks
On the inside
When I allow God to inspire
My heart and soul
My entire life and spirit
With belief that is so tender
On the inside . . .

The love that dances to life
On the inside
When I allow God to stir
The wonder of His adoration
His gift of affection
His blessings of protection
On the inside . . .

This hope, faith and love
From God above
On the inside of my heart
Where I know He is alive
Burning out a promise
That He will always keep me going!

Reflective Soul

I sit silently, so still
On the wooden chair in the den
Beside a window, sun raining in
Baptizing my thoughts
In warmth, blazing breaths
Of faraway wonders

The seat I sit upon
Once was a sturdy oak
Filled with dancing leaves
Sunshine purred through
Composing a song
Of detailed hopes, dreams
Pondered by graying
Branches so powerful
Cardinals and wrens convened
On them, a meeting
Heart, soul and mind
Chirping and crooning delight
As they while away the mornings

Reflecting on the mysteries
God's wisdom, His creativity
Smiling from a sun who gleams
Against a backdrop of ridges
Emerald and sapphire mountains
Peaks like the hands lifted
In prayer, praising Him
The Maker of their wrinkles
The Reason for the massifs
Who preach hope, faith and love
Mixed together with joy and peace

As I sit on my wooden seat
Echoing my heart
Grace promises me to listen
As I share my soul
Glorifying the One who knows
My thought are the thoughts of
The gladness of knowing
His rising Son, the only One
To bring true hope
For the yearning soul

In the shadows of the setting sun
His peace reveals the saving love
I long for, plead for, wait for
With each prayer my thoughts invoke

Just Believe

There are those who question
The reality of a God who knows us
One who smiles down on our confession
That the sin we might not discuss
Is still a dark and dreadful transgression

There are those who doubt
The need for His mercy and grace
They don't know what it's all about
Wanting for the Savior we embrace
Needing a redeemer to seek out

There are those who don't understand
The meaning of God's absolution
Refusing to listen to God's command
To repent and believe the solution
The One sitting at God's right hand

There are those who look for a reason
God's motive for giving His pardon
Believing this to be like high treason
Following the occurrence in the garden
When sin came to us in due season

There are those who don't want to believe
In spite of the truth—Jesus saves
They don't seem to know how to receive
Through faith that doesn't end at graves
But follows us to an eternity we'll never leave

There are those who won't enter paradise
With the hope that comes to hearts who know
God is alive inside because He paid the price
The highest price we could not pay, buy or borrow
He loved us all so much He became the sacrifice

I believe in Jesus Christ
Whose great sacrifice sufficed
Because of His gift, His life
We can live again without strife
Because of His light, His love
We can someday live up above
Because of His grace, His loss
We can bring it all to the cross!

God bless you with a new life!

Your Gift

*Use your gift to give back to the One who created us all,
loved our hearts and assured us of hope.*

—BY POET

We all, each one, have a gift to share
A gift from heaven, from God
Calling to us from our deepest prayer
A talent from His heart, His grace
A knack for giving back something so rare
It is like we are genius, offering
Joy, hope, peace beyond compare

We all, each on, have a gift designed
To be shared with everyone,
To be given, without remorse, to spellbind
The gentle spirit, the heart and soul
Of those who know that we have signed
A contract with heaven, a vow
To give our ability to the love defined

We all, each one, have a gift of grace
Poured out from God onto our hearts
So that we can always delight to embrace
The heart and soul of those who know
We are giving and will never erase
The wonders of His power, His light
Raining down on us a love to showcase

We all, each one, have a gift of life
To give back to the world all we have
Be it good deeds, artful things, midwife
We can share our gifts with others

Who need to feel the comfort from strife
That comes from believing and achieving
The way to share the promise of the afterlife

We all, each one, have a gift of love
Granted by the Creator who brings us
Each one of us the joy from up above
Reminding us that we are given the chance
To spend our lives with hope undreamed of
Because we're given the gifts He gives
Even though we might be unworthy of

We all, each one, have the gift He has given
And it is my prayer it is for God we'll be living

> *And there are diversities of operations, but it is the same God which worketh all in all. 7. But the manifestation of the Spirit is given to every man to profit withal.*
> —*1 Corinthians 12:6*

I Want Him to Know Me

I want Him to know
In the depths of my soul
He is alive, in full control

I want Him to see
The way He brings to me
Endless joy, hope and peace
Love that shines His light
All through me

I want Him to feel
The sincerity of my heart
A heart who believes
A heart who receives
The wonder of His Son
Love that won't be outdone

I want Him to realize
This compassion that is His
Gift to me, His answer
To those prayers I prayed
For His blessing—this is the answer
To my every prayer for acceptance

I want Him to understand
The way I need His grace
Poured out across my life
So that I dance with joy
From His amazing glory

I want Him to discern the truth
About my faith and my hope
It is His light, His love, His peace
That fulfill my life's every need

It is His affection and tenderness
That whisper into me such gentleness
It is His promise to never leave me
That brings me relief from fear
It is His presence that gives me
Assurance that I have been blessed

I want Him to know my thoughts
My heart and soul, my hopes
I want Him to know in my heart
There is love for Him that is alive
Surviving the tests of time
Enlightening, brightening, exciting
Praising Him with my entire life!

Fig Leaf

Concealed beneath a fig leaf,
Nakedness of more than body
Nakedness of heart and soul
Nakedness of darkened thought
Nakedness of the sinful doubt
Nakedness of screaming pain

They weren't prepared,
When they bit into the fruit . . .
For the fear that could consume
They weren't ready,
When they finally knew . . .
Evil was there where they lived
Sin was a heart wrenching
Penetrating dread, in the shadows
Where dusk fell against smooth skin
In whispers of silhouettes broken
Dreams riding the seas
The depths of hopelessness
Raining down shame
Humiliation and disgrace
Degradation that feeds on
The fig leaf we hold onto
As we struggle to cover up
Sins that are as black
As the night, only more appalling
More frightening

Secreted beneath a fig leaf,
Vulnerable and exposed
To the starkness of shame
The stubbornness of pride
The sinfulness that stirs minds
To listen to the fear, the dread

The naked ache that screams
For hearts to break

It is only a fig leaf
Covering the sin
Until God whispers grace
Across the naked stain
Reminding the heart
He died to reconcile us
To Him, the beginning and end

A Simple Prayer

Sometimes I simply whisper . . .
Help me, Jesus, please
Other times, I simply smile . . .
Thank you, Jesus . . .
I don't know the how or why
But I know You've blessed my entire life

Sometimes I just ask Him silently . . .
When will I see Your face?
He never answers the question
Though I know that He is there
Listening to my silent prayers
Giving me the strength to share
All my hopes, needs and cares
With the One who knows me best

Sometimes I humbly invite Him
To hear the way I've sought Him
And give me His voice, His grace
The joy that lives in His presence
But I never fail to be amazed
When I feel the way He rains down
Love that is rich and true, love
That is so alive, so fulfilling, so real
Love that is beyond my understanding
It's so alive—so wise, so blessed

It is this genuine love, this authentic
Feeling from His spirit, His gift to us
The grace that frees my soul to pray
The mercy that penetrates my thoughts
The kindness that comes from His light . . .
Filling my heart and soul with hope
My mind with complete peace and thanks

For all the tenderness that He brings
Such love, such anointing, is my comfort
My joy flows so abundant . . . inspiring me
To give my heart to the One I know
Holds the key to my very soul, the One
Who brings me through the worst that comes
Into a life that He's blessed with His virtue

With all my heart and soul, I praise Him
The answer to all my fears and tears
The light who pours love through the years

With God, I have everything I ever needed
Every blessing that I could even think of
The inspiration to share my heart and soul
As they dance through the wonders growing
From His gift of such a brilliant reflection
Of all that He's created, all that He's given
To His children . . . the ones He loves completely
With a love that is beyond comprehension

He Is My Everything

His light is gentle
A caress, a sensitive presence
Pouring out hope on the heart
Mercy on the spirit,
Grace on the soul who knows
He is alive on the inside
Of the heart who believes

His laughter is sincere
A joy, penetrating feelings
Raining down from heaven
Pleasure that is beyond words
It sings and dances, fulfills
The spirit with its wonder
Its ability to inspire serenity

His love is the answer
To prayers for contentment
Lingering on the heart and soul
Who know that His love grows
More potent, more alive
With each passing smile, each
Gift of His shining light

His light, laughter and love
Pour out hope, peace and faith
Unending joy and grace
A new beginning, a fresh way
To reach beyond the worry
Discover the music inside a feeling
Brought to life by the spirit
Who knows God is the tenderness
Found inside the soul who knows
God is the answer to every hope

The remedy for every hurt
The satisfaction in the love

He is the answer to our problems
He makes a way where there was no way
He is the promise that life is good
Because He is the God who created us
With love that is so amazing . . .

It is a love that assures every doubt
He is the way, the truth, the life
He is the answer to the prayer I pray
For someone to strengthen me
With assurance that there is a way
To breath love into every dark place
His love revives our hearts and souls
With a joy that is complete and assured!

God of Angel Armies

God of angel armies
Rain down Your hope and joy
Fill our lives with your kindness
Peace that raises our belief
To the knowing that love is alive
Coloring our hearts and our lives
In hues of beauty and grace
Inspiration that feels like an embrace
Your presence enchanting the spirit
Breathing wonder through the feelings
Baptizing souls in endless brilliance
Like sun pouring out her wisdom
Moonlight reflecting heaven's genius
Stardust luminating wildest dreams

God of angel armies
Remind me why I am here today
A part of the human race, a child
Of the living God, who I praise
For His compassion, His gentleness
His blessings that encourage
My soul to linger on the shores
Where oceans roar and waves toss
Powerful, piercing the darkness
Reassuring minds of insights, strong
Longings caressing thoughts, ideas
With flames of passionate desires
Fires of promises, raging words
Freeing the muse to give back
To this old world, a piece of the heart
Songs of sincerity, serenity, sensitivity
Signs of the Savior's love glowing
Flowing through veins of existence
Tenderness gripping the intimate truth
Of a feeling, thriving on His love

God of angel armies
Flourishing, growing, stirring
All the glory that is Yours, Your
Wonder, Your beauty and peace
Your forever gift . . . The Son
Who brings absolute peace, saving
Hearts from the darkness, the disgrace
The shame and dishonor, the humiliation
The ultimate destruction of hell's fury

God of angel armies
I praise You for Your mercy
Your lasting love and grace
Your gentleness and kindness
Your never ending forgiveness
Your joy, hope and contentment
The Wonder that is Your truth
Poured out over hearts who need You!

> *Turn us again, O Lord God of hosts, cause thy face to shine; and we shall be saved.*
> *—Psalm 80:19*

But God

I know I don't do everything right
I want to be perfect, but am so inadequate
I want to be flawless, but am so very flawed
I want to be impeccable and am so deficient

But God . . .
I try to do it all just so
I'm weak and I know I do so much wrong
But God . . . I try so very hard
To do what I know You would have me to
To do what is right in the eyes of Your truth
To do what is good and kind and wise
To do what I know Your word tells me to

But God . . .
I am so very lacking, so fallible and weak
I struggle to show You the best that I have
I try to give You my unsurpassed love and light
Hope that will show You how much I need You
To feel the way I love You from the depths of my spirit

But God . . .
I know I'm so imperfect
I do things wrong even when I don't want to
I let pride and prejudice get in my way sometimes
I allow the pain and sorrow to take my heart away from
The place where I can be closest to You

But God . . .
You just have to know my heart
And see that I love You more with every thought
I need You and I praise You and I pray that You know
It is Your love that lights my heart and soul
It is Your love that assures me of this hope

But God . . .
You are the reason I can honestly say
I may not be perfect, but I'm someone who strives
To give back to You a heart that is honest and true
A heart that knows Your worth and reflects the blessing
Of Your gift of grace and mercy, Your absolute love and affection
Toward a child like me who knows they will be defective until
The time when I reach the home of my Savior
Where His love will remind me I have the victory
Success comes in the form of a meeting in heaven!

But God . . .
Please don't ever leave me or forsake me
Without You, dear God . . . I'd be lost in the darkness
It is Your light that pours out hope into my heart,
Joy into my soul and love into my spirit!

But God . . . .
I love You with everything in me!

Forever Flying

Spring whispers joy into the spirit
Promises of hope sing from wildflower
Melodies, reflecting brilliant smiles
Falling down from moonlit skies

Spring breathes laughter into the heart
Inspiration over the silence of a thought
Prayers compel the soul to feel His peace
Pouring over the life of those He feeds
With His bread of life, with His liquid calm
Caressing every sigh with kindness so rare
So faithful and precious it shines, sparkling
Stunning pearls of starlight dreams, grace
Lingering on the one who knows He is alive
His praises are the way we still the shadows
With worship restoring the blessing that
Has faded into the moments of darkness
When litanies grew braver and more certain
That God would sanctify the broken heart
Who comes to Him for healing, fulfillment
Gentle touches of restorative rebuilding
His grace is the light of our freedom
From fears, tears and years of disgrace
Shame that reflects all the ways we've been
Pulled away from the Creator, His Son,
Our life and love and living salvation who knows
Hearts and souls, above and below, He knows
All that we are and all that we hope and pray
He knows our deepest thoughts, our music
That sings thanks across the heavens
And awakens therapeutic insights, ideas
Love that is alive, dancing on the inside
Heartening our belief and preparing us to be
Followers of the One who bled and died
So we could live with His spirit on the inside

Spring is a touch of grace praising heaven's Son
The One who makes a way where there seems to be
No way—all seems dark, lost and alone, without even
A chance to be won and He knows the way to take
To bring redemption from a little faith, just a faith
That is the answer to our heart's worst fears, tears
Those solitary glimpses into the sadness we feel
When we let His love fade into the background of our
Thoughts, our faith, our thanks . . .

Spring comes to life when we realize He is alive
On the inside where we can always know He is prepared
To hear and answer our yearnings, our prayers
With a love that is louder than the strongest winds
Love that is colored in hues of promise and praise
Unending faith that leaves only the faded memory
Of pain or grief because He is there, giving His best,
At the slightest thought, the least request . . .

Spring reminds me why I will never really die
Death will come in the Winter of my life
But I know the Son who has given me this hope
Of a Springtime when my soul shall fly
In the beauty of a heavenly sky, alive—forever flying!

I Am Weak, But He Is Strong

I'm weak but He is strong
I'm lacking but He is all
I'm but a shadow falling in His light
His grace reminds me that love is alive
Inside the one who He has forgiven
One who follows His teaching and heeds His word
Listens to the whisper of kindness that inspires
Hearts to be stirred and souls to be on fire
For the One who is a guide to everyone who does abide
In the love that is salvation to the believer, the disciple
Of this Son, this King of Kings, this Savior born of love

I'm so fragile but He is fervent
I'm filled with fear but He is my courage
I'm like a faded flower in the field
While He is like a bright and resilient bloom
Thriving amid the faintest blossoms, beautiful
His grace pouring out joy through the soul
Who knows His love just grows and grows
Blessing those who know His mercy and generosity
Are part of the reflection of a compassion so alive
It silences doubt and keeps kindness raining down
On the heart of each believer, each one who knows
He is the way, the truth and the life—He is the bright
And morning sun, the dawn of a new life, a clean slate
A new start that will give a second chance to share faith

I'm so frail but He is so powerful
I'm nothing at all without Him and His gift
Of grace that glorifies His Holy name, with thanks
For the One who has given us everything
His heart, His love, His life and hope from above
Assuring the spirit that He will always be with me
A light penetrating the darkest dread, comforting

The soul who is fearful and anxious, worried about things
That only God who tells us to never worry can know about
Little things and big things, troublesome parts of life
That keep us bothered by concerns, the worst strife
But reminds the heart that prays that they need to say
One more prayer of faith, prayed from the soul of the one
Who believes and receives the comforting peace of grace
Poured out on hearts who listen to God's reassurance
His help is but a prayer away and all we need to do is say . . .

Dear God, please help . . . make a way
His *love and grace* will not delay

Godly Women

Some are mothers, reflections of love
Poured out on children who abide in hope
Remembering that Mary, the mother of Jesus,
Gave us all a sense of the wonder uncovered
By the women who give their hearts to children

Some are wives who give their husbands
Their hearts, their blessings, their kindness
Like Ruth, the Moabite, who was great-grandmother
To the King after God's own heart, David,
Who played such a great role in the lineage of Jesus

Some are followers of the King of Kings
Those who know He is the best there is
Believers who give their entire lives to Him
Like Mary Magdalene, who Jesus healed and who
Was also the first witness of His resurrection

Some are women who love with all they have
Through joy and pain, in spite of everything
Giving all their lives to their beloved
Like Rachel who knew what is was to be childless
Sharing her beloved with her sister, Leah

Some are women who have a desperate yearning,
Like Hannah, who yearned for a child of her own
She prayed, promising to give her son back to the Lord
When Samuel, her son, anointed King David,
He gave the entire world a new direction toward redemption

Some are women who fall into great sin
Like Eve, the mother of Cain and Abel
She was deceived by the enemy of us all,
And changed the entire fate of mankind
Including the way we would live in this life

Some are like Deborah, who was a judge of her time
Others, like Esther, who changed the heart of the King
Some are like Miriam, prophetess and Moses' sister
Others, like Sarah, who had Isaac at 90 years of age
Some are like Elizabeth, who bore John the Baptist.
Then, there is Priscilla, who was a powerful church leader
Also, there was Mary who was sister of Lazarus
And, Martha who was rebuked by Jesus so her sister,
Mary, could sit at the Master's feet and hear His words

All the women of the Bible were strong and blessed
By the One who gave each one of us the chance to have
A personal relationship with Jesus, our Lord and Savior
The One who taught all women that they could be a light
Guiding others through the darkness, into His grace

Praise God for women of the Bible and women of today
Who share the faith that Jesus is the only way!

The Final Journey

Grace rains down on the one who listens
Hearing the sound of His glorious spirit,
His amazing words call out for heeding
His gentle song breathes love into the soul
Of the one who knows He is filled with this
Everlasting grace, hope that knows no despair
Light that knows no darkness—it shines brighter
Than the morning sun, like a fire from the One
Who God calls His precious Son, the only One
Who was willing to give His life for love!

As I journey through this world, my heart notes
The splendor of His creation and the love
That colors hearts in praise, prayer and promises
Pure, penetrating pleasure raining down on those
Who know He is the soul's greatest blessing,
The caress of an awesome Creator, our Savior

Along my way, as the journey brings such grace,
I feel His light pouring out on me with a faith
That is alive—it is brighter than the moonlight
More magnificent than stardust thoughts who dream
Of shadows filled with His kindness, His peace
The beauty of His unending mercy and sympathy
He is alive in the sound of each wind whispering
Joy through the one who knows He is the compassion
Filling up the heart with such appreciation and gladness

His spirit leads the way on this path of gentle prayers
Praise of the Savior who enlightens and accepts us
All our faults and flaws, the sins we can't pretend to ignore,
All of us—our worst and our best, the pieces of our quest,
Are known by this wonderous love who pours out on us
Blessings that can never be measured, redemption, peace

And hope that never leaves . . . on this journey through life
I know that His saving grace is the only thing that I can take
To that place where I journey toward, that heavenly home
Where His love smiles down through the wonder of a love
That lives on and on, a love that is forever, eternal, always

Love like this knows no fears, no tears . . . only hope and faith
The miracle of grace that never fades, grace that awakens
The heart to praise like they've never been away from the home
Where the journey ends and we, like Jesus, can say, . . .

"It is finished"

Everyday, in Every Way

Everyday, I need to pray
For God's will to lead me through
Color my thoughts in hues of
Kindness, hope, generosity
Breathe laughter and light
Through my spirit, embracing
With whispers of gentleness
Caressing my heart with such
Amazing tenderness—It could
Only be given by a God so alive
He fills up my soul and shines His
Love on the inside, sparkling
With excitement and insight

Everyday, I need to say
God, I love You. I hear what you say
I'll listen to Your truth raining down
From the heavens, where You are living
A light filling up every soul who believes
That You are here inside, where You
Will never leave—You're forever
Aware of my needs and fulfilling my
Every desire with Your holy fire
Your kindness and grace, Your understanding
The goodness that is Your nature!

Everyday, I need a way
To give back to You, my eternal hope,
The One who answers all my prayers
The One who quiets my fears
The One who wipes away my tears
The One who builds a bridge of faith
Between my heart and Your everlasting
Grace, Your love and peace, Your joy

And the wonder of Your gift to me
The Gift of a Savior who made a way
For me to speak to You, my God
The One who gives my heart a home
The One who lets me know I'm never alone
The One who is the answer to my prayers
The One who is life to my heart and soul

Everyday, in every way, I need to say
I love You, God, and I'll always need You
To fill my life with Your kindness and spirit,
Your complete peace and penetrating joy

Thank You, God . . . for all that You've given me

Knowing God

Whispers of faith rain over my heart
Reminding me why I'm here, I'm alive
Feeling the joy and delight of knowing
His love is here inside, breathing hope
Into my soul, where I can always know
The light that shines down from heaven
Is filled with inspiration, kindness, grace
Wonders so beautiful they imitate the
Praise that frees my thoughts and mind
With admiration, adoration, devotion
For the One who makes my life so bright
It feels like love has colored the skies

Serenity so soothing it seems to embrace
My thoughts, my feelings, my belief, my dreams
With jewels of elation freeing me from fear
Assuring my heart that I'm forever His
Child of the King, believer and receiver
Follower of Jesus, the way, the truth, the life
The One who brings me forgiveness for sin
And fills my soul with a brilliant assurance
That He is always there for me, faithful,
Praiseworthy, the answer to my every prayer
For hope that uplifts and cheers my heart
With kindness that knows He brings satisfaction.

Prayers are lifted to spark His insight
Into the moment, the position, the heart
Who needs His love, His light, His kindness
Poured out on the appeal for His tenderness
His gift of grace, His inspiration and empathy
The miracle of the love that He brings
To every need, each request, every blessing
All the feeling that comes alive inside
The soul who knows His unconditional love!

With every thought, each moment, all that comes
There is the blessing of His captivating hope
His enchanting faith and His charismatic love
Flowing through the veins of those who know
His blood covers every sin, each offence, all wrong
With the purity of His everlasting sacrifice
For the ones who believe in Him through it all
Give back to Him their hearts who know He is
The answer for us all, the light in the darkness
The joy that lives in the soul who knows Him.

Joy in the Morning

Glorious dawn, morning sun
Rising high, high, higher
In a gentle cerulean sky
Awakening the earth to promises
Fresh moments, new thoughts
Raining down inspiration, joy
To hearts who know His love
Grows stronger inside the one
Who feels His presence, alive,
Inside the sunrise, the birth
Of a new day, a new way
A new kind of hope penetrating
The silence of daybreak

Wonderful dawn, first hope
Painting the moments in delicate
Light, soft glow of a rising sun
Soaring across the silence of a sky
Blazing with promises, vows
Gentle embraces from the winds
Who whisper faith on the feelings
Blended with soul soothing serenity
Sensations of sensitivity and comfort
Breaths of melody, songs, psalms
Grace poured out on the soul who knows
He is life, abiding on the inside
Where He knows my every thought
Each word I speak, everything known
To my soul—He knows and He shows
My heart the way to complete peace

Holy Spirit Fire

Holy Spirit, dancing fire . . .
Quiet my heart, blaze through my life
Igniting flames of hope, flames of joy
Flames of exhilaration, flames of grace
Flames of inspiration to fill up my soul
With the amazing wonder that is Your
Spark glowing through my life, burning
Paths of expectations, promises, faith
Born of a Holy Fire, dancing a waltz
Of sacred love raining down from higher
Above where God sits on His throne

Holy Spirit, painting my entire world . . .
With breathless rays of pleasure,
Rising up from the joy of knowing
God is inside my soul, restoring my dreams
Reassuring my desires, exciting a fire
Penetrating yearnings for more of the love
That is more glorious than I can describe
More beautiful and wise than any kindness
It is a love that is alive, like the rays of
A Son who knows our hearts, minds and souls
Provides us with forgiveness for our sins
Shows us the way to belief that is filled with
Second chances, renewal and grace that prays
For spiritual completion, God's redemption

Holy Spirit, fire of my heart . . .
Pour out Your joy through my entire life
Make me into someone who understands
Someone who listens to all Your wisdom
With comprehension who knows Your counsel
Is better than any guidance I will ever have
Your suggestions are alive with passion

And overflowing with boundless grace
Peace that knows no darkness or dread
Kindness that is more brilliant and sensitive
Than the sparkling stardust delights
Of a gentle, starry night filled with moonlight

Holy Spirit, fervor of my soul . . .
Whisper Your compassion through my thoughts
Fill me up with kindheartedness, gentleness
Peace that surpasses all understanding
A melody that is like a psalm from the scriptures
Prudent and patient, promising a Savior
Who brings deliverance from the shadows
Of sorrow, pain and disappointment
All the things that are stalked through the darkness
Where dread and despair destroy the light
Shining bright from the heart of One
Who knows our hearts and our thoughts, our all
Loves us beyond our wildest imaginings
With a love that is sure, saving, sincere
Love that has no conditions, no fears
Love that is the answer to every prayer
Love that is from a spirit who comes to us
Lives in us, brightening our lives, breathing
His Holy Spirit fire into our souls!

Hope Inspires

Hope came to life inside my soul
When I realized I'd been saved to the uttermost
By the One who lived then died on a tree
So that I could know Him as the light of love
Who shines bright, destroying every fear in my heart

Hope awakened a joy within my spirit
When I comprehended the news that I was someone
Who had found the light of a love, a wonder
Beyond any description, any knowing, anything
He is more sure than the moon and stars, the sun
Cannot shine brighter than His pure, sweet love

Hope stirred within my heart where I met Him
The One who is a promise, a prayer, a psalm, forever
My inspiration, my kindness, my reflection of belief
In the light who prepares my heart for the freedom
That comes to life inside the soul who knows His grace
His whisper of love giving second chances, redemption
Love that is stronger than the sun's reflections
Raining down joy that uplifts and feeds the spirit
With an adoration, an affection, that abides on the inside
Of the heart who knows that He is God's light
And, He is life and love—He is the joy from above

Hope rouses the feelings of elation within my heart
Because I know the One who is filled with sweet love
He inspires my thoughts to listen to His words
Believe in the promises that He has left me with
Lingering in the waters of His amazing, lasting grace
The blessing of a love that is filled with assurance
That He will always be there, just beyond a prayer
Where I know He will reveal His kindness, His care
And reassure my spirit that He will always be there

Hope silences all my fears and reminds me why I can say
I am blessed beyond my wildest dreams, with blessings
That penetrate my spirit with feelings of God's power
His overwhelming gentleness, tenderness and relieves me
Of every sorrow, each dread, all the worry that brings distress
He reminds me that I am loved and I can live on these prayers
To the One who makes a way where no way has ever been
The One who guides my heart through the darkest dread
And assures me that I am loved much more than I can comprehend

Hope spoils every damaging word, all darkness, all alarm
With a feeling of His light pouring through the hearts
Who know Him as Savior and believe He has been alive
Within the spirit of those who know His love is prepared
To strengthen every spirit with kindness, peace and love
That comes to life inside the heart who knows this light
Reflects the wonder of a life who gave us so much more
Than we could possibly ever thank Him for . . . He gave us
A second chance, forgiveness, a way to come to terms
With all the sorrows, regret and disillusionment that remind
Our lives are His, paid for with a price that was higher
Than any price we could have paid . . . with Him, there is
A true and living grace that awakens spirits to the assurance
That Jesus is alive, living with us, living within us!
And, I hope He knows the way that I praise Him!

Camping with Jesus

Nursing dreams around a campfire
Bleeding inspiration through the smiles
Laughter like blessings raining down
On the hearts who share this sweetness
A whisper of dreamy wonder twinkling
Like stars who wink from the night sky
From their home on high, above a world
Of music, songs drifting on winds
Healing hopes and faith completed
By the impressions of praise, prayers
Psalms guiding graceful light upon
Moon breathed intimacy of the dusk
Who lingers on the ridges of mountains
Colored in hues of blessings, miracles
Alive, dancing wildly in the campfire
Time for promises to become authentic
Realities of love embracing the soul
Who knows that this is the moment
This is the day, the time, the grace
Of Him who lights up the heart, the soul
With dreams, visions, reveries—creativity
Full blown love overflowing the Son's
Gentle touch from a night who is alive
With firefly thoughts and glittery legends
Luminating the skies with a life that is better
Than any treasure, any wealth, any plunder

It is the height of summer, camping
By the creek, listening to the meek exposes
Flowing along, creating ripples in clear, cool streams
Where fish and children play like hearts
On fire for the lapping sprays of delicious liquid
Freshening, fulfilling, flavoring the heart
With ambiances of delicious whispers, echoes

Shrieking out greetings from the glow
Of a silent affection who knows our deepest yearnings
Our wishes turned upside down, covered in tenderness
Warring with the darkness who fades in and out
Shadowing the firelight with a moon who sighs peace
Trapping intimacy in the face of a known belief
Who is Jesus embracing the spirit from His kindness
Bleeding through the night like a rush of rapids
Engulfing the gentle waters in that hastening stream

It is His love that pours out hope and peace, joy and faith
Love that penetrates the weakest part of the spirit
With a brilliant flame of inspiration, coloring the heart
The vision with a delicate love who listens to His wisdom
And glows like the campfire, falling in silhouettes
Of beauty and peace across a spirit alive with His grace

Inside My Soul

I whisper a quiet prayer
Gentle thoughts of hope and faith
Inspirations for the one who knows
God is alive and He is up above
Yet He is inside, sharing His insights
Filling my soul with His wonder
His light and love, His second chance
To be someone worthwhile
Someone who knows God as guide

I murmur a tender prayer
Soft reflections of beauty and peace
Dreams awakened by the Father
Who shares His kindness, His compassion
The joy of a smile, a twinkle in an eye,
The feeling that this life is simply
A stepping stone on the way to much more
The assurance of a place where His
Love fills the entire abode with rapturous joy

I breathe a personal prayer
With promises that will not fade
Into the shadows of worry or pain
These treasured assurances remind
That His light will always stir the belief
Bringing out feelings of absolute relief
Reassurance that His grace, His way
Is the answer to every need, each plea
For a new day, a new way, bringing
Hearts into the relationship that assures
His love is stronger than we can imagine
His love is filled with the delight of heaven

I sigh an authentic prayer
Filled with the desire to spark a fire
Of joy that warms the heart and soul
With the promise of a love that is a sign
From above—a light in the darkness
Shelter from the storm and so much more
This love comes to life inside the one
Who knows that life only begins
When we're forgiven of our sins
By the One who knows our spirits
And secures our souls with His redemption

I'm thankful for the One who created me
And gave me His spirit to inspire this faith
That will always be alive and filled with delight
Because I know the One whose spirit resides inside.

A Christian Thank You

Thank You, God, for your grace
For your joy, hope and peace
Thank You for the way You change
Hearts from hard to hearts who
Believe in a love that is alive inside
Where Your spirit overshadows
All the hardness—the loathing
That comes from a heart who
Doesn't truly know Him, a heart
Who doesn't sincerely believe
That His Son, Jesus, was the One
To bring salvation to His people

Thank You, God, for Your wisdom
For Your light shining in the dark
Calming every worry, destroying
All the depression that tries to
Fill hearts with silhouettes of doubt
Feelings that cause a life to abound
With despair, dread and everything
That makes the heart feel so down

Thank You, dear God, for Your kindness
The warmth that You color our life with
The sweetness of a love that lingers inside
Where we can always know it will bring to life
Joy that overflows the doubt, wonder which
Allows the spirit to breath in the beauty
Of inspiration and imagination, peace that reflects
Whispers of astonishment and prayers
Filled with the knowledge of a light
Which never fades, a light that spreads
Its rays across the spirit, into the life
Of the one who listens to the sound of hope

Falling from the heavens where He gives out
Assurance that we have the answers to our prayers
In the One who gave us a second chance,
Forgiveness of our sins and a sincere confidence
Within where we can feel His love filling us up
With the spirit that is His gift—His hope
The wonder of His spirit guiding us to become
People who shine a light across the entire world

Relentless Love

Unending grace, relentless love
Poured out from the hand
Of a God who gives us all we need
Joy, hope and complete peace

He fills our hearts with eternity
Endless light reflecting our quiet
Elation, without any uncertainty
Euphoria dancing, gentle jubilation
Through our souls, across our lives
Reminding us to give generously
Love that is vibrant, colored in hues
Of kindness so astonishing it grows
Flowers of gratitude, thanksgiving
To the One who blesses to the uttermost

Magnificent mercy, like a beautiful song
Resonating affection, wonder and love
Thriving in the shadows of stardust wishes
Bold and brilliant rays of sunny adoration
Lifting wings of gracious elegance, fading
Into the edges of a dream so free to imagine
A belief that is sure, wise and filled with
Inspiration, adoration, praise of the Creator
Who brought us His everlasting compassion
Forgiveness of every sin, each iniquity
Every cloud of shame, doubt or dread

With love like His, we can always believe
Our hearts will be filled with reverence
For His wonderous gift, His amazing grace
The victory of a hope that is complete
Because it was erected on the cornerstone
The One and only Jesus Christ, the Son

Who gave every believer a new song, a new life
A second chance, a way to change, a freedom
To love with a heart who is filled with His spirit.

War's Words

Hearts are heavy, burdened
By worry and fear, a darkness
Coloring thoughts in dread
Breaking through hope and joy
To leave anxiety and concern
Panic about what might come

Hearts are scared, apprehensive
Wondering what might happen
To the world who is being consumed
By terror, shadows of gloom
Will war bring our fears into reality?
Our worries to an actuality?

Hearts are aware that the conflict
Has gone far beyond our assurance
There is catastrophic tragedy
Spoken of all through the world
Will this trouble condemn everyone?
To a battle no one can comprehend?

Hearts are nervous, agitated
By an alarm that dims the best dream
A dread that feels like it is murkier
Than the dirtiest, most dismal waters,
A dread that is so terrifying . . . .
Will this fight claim lives we know so well?

Will war bring an end to our heart's hopes?
Will we reach out to find all we love is gone?
Will our hearts know the answer to prayers . . .
Prayers only God can solve or bless . . .

Please pray for His help, His blessing, His grace
Pray for the chance to give Him all the praise!

Secreted in the Scriptures

Hidden in the scriptures
Are joys beyond measure
Hopes that can't be bought
Promises that restore hearts
Light of the word and soul
Wonders that bless the thoughts

Concealed there in the scriptures
Are boundless little reminders
That God is always wiser, kinder
More aware and more alive, higher
Than any dream or any need
He is the answer to everything

Secreted there in the scriptures
Are words that we can treasure
Delights that bestow understanding
Comprehension that comes to life
Inside the soul who hears His word
And believes beyond doubt or question

Buried there in the scriptures
Are verses that are more precious
Than any poetic idea or vision
These words are filled with vibrant
Healing, wisdom and complete belief
In the One who brings so much relief

Veiled there in the scriptures
Are insights into His implications
Ideas that bring love to life
Restore joy and destroy strife
Remind our hearts of the love inside
That is witness to the Son, Jesus Christ

Shrouded there in the scriptures
Are kindnesses and blessings
Poured out from the Holy Spirit
Who knows our needs before we do
And gives us the ultimate gift
Of faith that praises Him fully

When you read the scriptures
You will find the answers to prayers
The healing that makes you aware
God is forever a light in the darkness
A still, small voice who uplifts you
The wonder of love that fulfills you

Read the scriptures for hope, faith and love
That is brighter than the heavens above

He Is a Guiding Light

My heart fills up
With a light of pure joy
Peace in the knowing
That God's love is overflowing
Raining down from heaven
Assuring me of grace
Wonders that will never fade
Inspiration to meet each day
With praise for the Creator
Who always makes a way

My heart collects fragments
Of scripture, verse and insight
Into the heart of our Heavenly Father
The One who guides our lives
Shines His amazing light
Into the shadows that darken
Our dreams, our hopes, our feelings
With fear and anxiety, a dread
That whatever comes there will be
Darkness that doesn't flicker
Alive with the starlight glimmers
To remind us that love is alive
A fire in the midnight skies

My heart reflects on the marvels
Of a bright and shining sunrise
Who whispers its joy through those
Listening to the silence, the breath
Of a kindness who reveals the desire
For prayers that plead and implore
Our beautiful Savior for His grace
His amazing serenity and solemn hope
For moments spent with Him

Delighting in His love, praising with
Promises for the everlasting knowing
That He will always be with us
Never leaving, never forsaking
Always bread and living water, the answer
To any worry, all queries, each matter
In need of a miraculous touch
From the spirit of pure, sweet love

My heart longs for this relationship
Between Jesus and myself
A relationship built on prayer with
A heavy dose of scripture
Penetrating the mind and soul
With light that is like a gentle sun
Pouring out on the one who knows
Jesus is the bright fire inside
Who rejoices when we share His grace
When we remember to praise our Creator
And when we listen to His guidance

He is alive and He is a healer
He is wise and He is resilient
He is the way, the truth, the life
Who became the ultimate sacrifice.
I love Him with my entire being!

His Entire Life

His heart rains down kindness
Gentle whispers of grace and peace
Feelings blending both hope and faith
Light intense and brilliant, soothing
Away the darkness that bleeds
Worry and doubt, deception
From its shadows of dread, despair

His spirit showers us with joy
Pouring out wonder and laughter
Healing the pains and the sorrows
Awakening reflections of desire
Fires of tenderness, aflame with
Praise and prayer, victorious
Inspirations to color the whole life
In melodies of splendor, growing
Graciously, like a daisy who stirs
Gentle thoughts to be freed
From their homes in the meadows

His mercies are new every morning
Flowing down to us from heaven
Where He awaits those who know Him
As Father, the One who will love
Unconditionally, fully, completely
With a love that is stronger, more alive
More powerful than any love in life
It is like the mighty sun or moon
Breaking through the darkness
Stirring up glimmering radiance
Feelings of pure adoration, praise
Of the One who brings us calm
Tranquility that is like a fulfillment
Breathed out of the pores of One

Who knows us as His children,
Creations who He loved and brought
To life by His own breath, in
His own image—His work, ablaze
With passionate hopes, dreams
Alive like stars and stardust lives
Blended with flames of grace
And poured out on the darkness
So that light begins to penetrate
Casting love across the shadows
And stirring overwhelming promise
Of a love that is forever, eternal
In that home on high, where we
Will never even die . . . always alive
In the presence of His love, His light
The Son who made this all possible
With the gift of His entire life!

Love So Alive

Love this alive will always thrive
Like stardust light, shining, inviting
Sparkling through the skies
Silencing ever doubt, every cloud
With gentle peace, promises
Of joy that breaks through darkness
Coloring the heart in kindness
A brilliant, breathless inspiration

Love brought to life without strife
Like shadows of intimacy, insight
Delighting the mind, pouring out hope
Across the spirit who knows Him
The only One who makes a way for us
Where no way has ever been before
The heavenly spirit, the glorious Christ
Prince of peace, king of kings, Savior
Of broken hearts and broken dreams

Love like this—love built on His gift
Brightens the darkest shadows
Reminds us that we always have His love
To capture our thoughts in belief
Our hearts in the warmth of peace
Our souls in the beauty of grace
Our lives in the wonder of His embrace

Love like this—love so alive it thrills
The mind who listens to its gentle caress
The life who believes in the second chance
Brought to us by a hope more alive
Than any dream, any heart, any life
A hope for the moment when we praise
With absolute assurance that He gave

Every heart the light to shine its flame
Through the life who knows He is
The Son who makes a way for true love

Love like this—love that is forever His
Is a love that builds a prayer on the soul
Who gives Him the faith, the sincere belief
That whatever comes there will always be
A light to pierce the darkness, a light of love
Who grows more alive and more aware
More assured and more like a real prayer
With the passage of time, the victory that shines
Through the heart who knows He is alive!

Love like this—love so capable of giving peace
Is a love that comes from the Father of our hearts
The God who created us to live in His loving presence
And feel all the wonder of His inspirations
As they reveal the amazing truth about our Creator . . .
He is the way, the truth, the life . . . He is Jesus
Our shining light—our hope, insight and love's fire

Listen to the miracle poured out on our lives
He is the spark of serenity and absolute love . . . is where He abides!

In a Silent Prayer

In a silent prayer . . .
      My heart pleads
For the grace, the stirring
      Of His presence
His charisma, His spirit
      Falling across my soul
Reflecting His precious love

In a silent prayer . . .
      My mind contends
With His cherished spirit
      Please bring peace
Joy, hope and wisdom
      Rain down your light
Across my thoughts

In a silent prayer . . .
      My heart beseeches
For the power of His love
      His kindness and courage
The affection that grows
      In abundance, pure peace
Flowing from His blood

In a silent prayer . . .
      My mind entreats
For the song of faith
      Poured out on my soul
Sprinkling me with hope
      Brilliant and alive
Like His blessed life

In a silent prayer . . .
        My heart petitions
For a song of mercy
        Music from the heart
Who knows that love
        Is alive on the inside
Of those who know Him

In a silent prayer . . .
        My mind begs
For a grace so beautiful
        It lights the night
With its penetrating joy
        Its sincerity and wonder
Praising the God of heaven

In a silent prayer . . .
        My heart and soul declare
His love is the only essential
        The reason for our hope
The purpose of our faith
        The intention of our ways
When we lift our hearts to pray

Fear Not

Fear often calls my name
Murmuring doubts
Darkness and shame
Motioning to my heart
Dread that silences with blame
Where can I go . . .
To my Savior, I proclaim . . .

Fear is like a black horror
Angry and bitter
Lamenting like a deplorer
Silencing the hope
Dimming dreams of the adorer
Filling hearts with clouds . . .
Soon, God will restore her . . .

Fear falls on the mind
Assaulting it with uncertainties
It has surely maligned
The joy that comes from confidence
Abiding on the kind
Who believe with all their hearts
Love is designed . . .
To bring light to the darkness . . .
Restore and remind . . .
That fear is in the past
Where God has defined
Love as His pen . . .

Writing on the walls of the soul . . . making hearts whole!

> *Fear thou not; for I am with thee: be not dismayed; for I am thy God: I will strengthen thee; yea, I will help thee; yea, I will uphold thee with the right hand of my righteousness.*
> —Isaiah 41:10

The Light of Friendship

With a heart full of hope
My smile spreads the whispers
Of thoughts so brilliant
Inspirations and visions clinging
To the music of a kindness
Brought to life by my insight
Comprehension of a experience
A moment in time, a sigh
Silence brought alive on the night
Within the spirit who denies
Brokenness or sorrow, pain
That shadows their heart, imagines
These gestures of faith portray
A second chance, a new day
The way toward joy and renewal
Hope . . .

With a heart full of light
Caressing the stardust dreams
Igniting the faith and peace
Bursting through the worries
The needs—fears and laments
Mourning that will only believe
Ballads howling grief, darkness
Poured out on the feelings
Who need only be graced by the
Reflections of promises, revelations
Throwing praise hovering on the skies
Emptying the mind of its ties
To anguish, aching disgrace
Suffering that fades to a dance
With fate

With a heart full of gentle faith
There comes the vibrant dream
Of life beyond grief and pain
Life that is lived in the presence
Of a Savior who makes every hurt
Seem like it will be extinguished
By His amazing love, His compassion
The feeling of absolute escape
From every darkness, each dreadful
Trouble or concern, every angst
Through His love there comes a calm
A quiet light that falls soft against
The moment, the day, the time
When hearts seem to be fighting
For a opportunity to reach out with hope
Find the warmth that covers the heart
With a pure, sweet love beyond dreams
A love so amazing it bleeds light into
The one who needs to know this is
God's gift, come to life inside the prayer
For a heart who is giving and living
To color someone's life in tenderness

With a heart who gives and listens
To the one who is in need, the one who grieves
There comes assurance that Jesus is
Alive inside, giving His answers through this friendship

Love Letter

I might not always tell you
But I hope you always know . . . .
You are my life's best blessing
You are the gift to my soul

I know I may not remember
To reveal my heart and soul
But when I think of You, dear Jesus
It is with assurance so bold
Bright and vibrant joy, wonder
Faith that never needs question
A light that thrives and survives
Each reflection, issue or doubt
A trust that lives in the silence
Of a gentle, calming touch . . .
From Your brilliance and perfection

I might not always let you know
Just how deeply I love you . . .
But I believe You can read my soul
And understand the feelings
That bloom beneath the shadows
Of Your kindness, Your tenderness
The beauty of Your grace
The miracle of Your inspiration
The love that makes my life complete

I know this love I feel for You
Is a love that is filled with praise
A love that leads me to worship
With joy, hope and sweetest faith
Love that is wise and warm
Abides on the heart who always knows
Jesus is the living water, the One
Who delights in this eternal love

I know that I may forget to say it
But the whisper of light from above
Pours heartfelt compassion and favor
Across this soul who knows that You
Are the answer to every single prayer
The warmth that comforts and cares
The love that never fades or goes away

With You, dear Jesus . . .
I can honestly say that this love
Will forever grow more wonderful
You are the One who brings my faith
Its assurance that I must praise
With a heart that believes and is grateful.

I Love Him

He blessed my whole world
With joy, peace and hope
Love that kindles the wonder
Coloring the skies in grace
Stirring the glory in praise
The brilliance in a sunny day

He blessed my whole heart
With a song of sincere light
Breaking through the verse
To warm spirits with kindness
Reflections of pleasure inside
The soul who believes in Him

He blessed my whole life
With a promise of gentle peace
Washing all of creation
In compassion, courage and confidence
That comes to life on the heart
Who knows He is their entire life

He blessed my whole soul
With a miracle found in prayer
For the ones who need His love
Abiding with them—within them
Flourishing in the beauty of One
Who gave His life to forgive our sins

He blessed my whole mind
With creativity and caring
Reminders of why I'm alive
Why I give and continue to share
The story of a man who gave me
Everything I would ever need

He gave me His understanding
He gave me His peace and caring
He gave me His acceptance
He gave me His forgiveness
He gave me His grace and mercy
He gave me His wisdom
And even though I'm so unworthy
He gave me His gift of salvation

Throughout life and eternity—I love Him!

He Is Worthy

When it comes from the heart
There is a whisper of insight
Soft feelings pouring out hope
Gentleness breathing light
Across the moments, the smiles
Of joy promised by His love

When it comes to the grace
Experienced at the edge of faith
There is kindness that brings awake
All the music discovered in praise
The brilliance of a song so alive
It colors the darkest sky in wonder

When it comes from the soul
There is compassion that is in control
Breaking through the silent dreams
Into the sensations of pure peace
Inspiration that is like a comfort
To the one who knows His encouragement

When it comes to the prayer
Of a heart who sincerely cares
There is satisfaction in the belief
Of the One who brings eternity
To the spirit who sincerely believes
Relying on the One who is life to me

When it come from the passion
Of a life who gives God the thanks
For His undying love and sweet grace
His light falling through the darkness
Reflecting all the beauty and insight
That comes from knowing Jesus' love

When it comes to the resurrection
There is a miracle of pure affection
Feelings brought to life by discernment
Into the marvelous love that ignites
A fire of adoration and sincere worship
Of this Lord who makes life worth it

When it comes from the nature
Of a love that abides on the inside
Praising and praying and stirring
All the feelings that God has moved
To life on the soul of those who choose
The One who brings absolute truth

When it comes to the final hours
As death brings its darkness to guide
The heart and soul from this world
Into the hereafter, where His light
Reflects all the wonder, the fulfillment
Of a love that comes from His gift

The gift of grace and faith and life
That abides in the love of Jesus Christ
Is like a sigh from paradise, a yearning
From the soul who knows He is worthy!

Keeper of the Flame

As churches close their doors tight
Walking away from the penetrating grace
Reigning down on hearts and souls
Who know God's love brings the fuel
To light the candle, the blazing flame
Of faith that will never go away

As people begin to lose their hope
Leaving the steadfast joy and peace
Felt by those who listen to His word
Preached by those who know He is
With us, within us, leading us to be
Guiding lights, salt of the earth

As tears fall silent against smooth skin
Weakening wills who have promised
Their praise of the Father who lives
Far away, in the heavens, where love grows
More alive, more potent, than it has
Ever been before—trickling gentle sobs

As shadows darken the brilliance
Of a light so alive, so tender and willing
To give the heart a part of God's mercy
Filling up thoughts with His loveliness
Singing soft whispers of promises
There abides a spark, glowing like wildfire

As life takes us to new places, new dreams
There are pieces of our senses, our beliefs
Flickering, quiet embers—of prayers, faith
Believing that His light is always there, alive
Living within the spirit where He is a friend
The keeper of the flame—redemption's gift

World Peace

Bring your thoughts to Jesus
Let Him silence all your doubts
Place your faith in His kindness
He is filled with mercy and hope
Allow Him to encourage your heart
With His grace, His joy, His peace
Feel the warmth of His gentle way
Healing all your worries and pains

Bring your yearnings to Jesus
Let Him fill you up with assurance
That love found in His presence
Is love that can destroy all mistrust
Freeing the soul from its past sins
Reassuring that light will shine again
Giving the seeker a second chance
To quiet all fears and wipe all tears
With the love that is forever awing

Bring your wars to this Jesus
Let Him know how you truly feel
Know that His love can destroy
All the darkness that shadows
The world with destruction, dismay
Despair that disgraces every chance
You are given to love unconditionally
With a heart and soul who believes
This Jesus fills the humble heart
With unending peace and serenity

Bring your worries, your discouragement
To the king of kings, the maker of dreams
The light of the world, the keeper of hope
Allow Him to show you the way to discover

A peace that is alive, like a fire inside,
Healing all the sorrow and revealing wonders
Alive inside the one who knows He is . . .
The answer to every prayer, the giver of life
The whisper of grace fulfilling our faith
With a love that comes alive on the inside
Of the one who knows that this light He shines
Is a light that will destroy all hate or loathing
Bringing kindness out of the shadows of aversion
Reminding the heart that His love is alive
And it is thriving inside the one who loves Him

Bring your battles to the One who knows the heart
And fills up the soul with the strength it needs
To end all war with a love that heals every wound!

He Is Alive

I look up toward the azure sky
Watch the flight of birds flying high
Soothing my dreams with light
Pouring over the stardust silence
Of a warm and tender moment

I smile at the whispers of life
Coloring my hopes in soft promises
Gentle tears raining down
Singing of beauty, laughter, insight
Into the spirit who listens
To the wonder of those who know
He is with us, fulfilling us
With His assurance, His comfort
His everlasting promise
Of a love that is alive, a fire
Burning through the heart who desires
A love that thrives on prayer
Survives because of the praise
That fills life with blessings
Thanks to the God of heaven

I look toward the amber dawn
Awakening on the softest thought
Weathering the darkest storm
Glowing on the heart who knows
His love is a forever warmth
The kindness of a bliss so hopeful
It dreams with peace eternal
Grace that brings such certainty
Of light that survives all worry
Comes alive on the serenity of glory
Who knows that love is much more
Than the whisper of a yearning

The gentleness that sooths away
Pain, anxiety and disgrace, the shame
Felt by the soul who knows that love
Is beckoning to the heart who shows
That its joy comes from the hope
Of a love that forever grows
Like the garden who is nurtured
By rain falling on its surface

When God rains down His joy
There is hope beyond any other
Hope of the light that will cover
Hearts in goodness, glory, grace
A feeling of unending faith
Thriving on the soul who believes
Jesus is alive and He is everything!

With Prayer

With prayer,
I discover the light
Of a love so astounding
It fills me up with hope

With prayer,
I find the answers
To those questions which
Remind me I am so imperfect

With prayer,
I realize the satisfaction
Of my dreams, my needs
Can be found in His arms

With prayer,
I uncover the joy that comes
From abiding in His sweet love
Learning from His glorious touch

With prayer,
I determine the reasons that peace
Comes to those who listen to His word
Find their mercy within the scriptures

With prayer,
I detect the meaning of grace
The unending wonder of a sincere blessing
Coming to those who sing His praises

With prayer,
I encounter the calm in the storm
The spark of joy just beyond the darkness
The melody that awakens His spirit within

With prayer,
I discern the meaning of my faith
The giving and trusting and acceptance
The kindness that pours from His heaven

With prayer,
I learn that love is all I really need
To honor this Jesus who I will always praise
With my spirit, my heart, my best thanks

With prayer,
I unearth the miracle of His salvation
The beauty in the One who never forsakes
The reason that I will always be protected

With prayer,
I acquire the answers to all my needs
I find the love of a friend who is everything
This Jesus makes intercession for me
So that I can see all the solutions to my worries
Know all the satisfaction of salvation
Because His blood washes me completely clean
And His love restores me to being a child of the King!

Saved by Grace

Tender light falls soft against my skin
Reflecting the inspiration
Of a heart who knows of Christ's gentle gift
Sincerity, serenity and sensations
Of silent reveries, grace so fulfilling
His healing is a comfort with its uplifting
Hope lingering on the silence
Like a smile twinkling in the eyes
Precious as stardust wonder pouring
From a sky ablaze with sparkling insight
Into the music of His wonderful mystery

His poetry sings, breathlessly,
Restoring the sound of mercy and prayer
Spoken by the soul who knows Him
As master, creator, king of the whole world
The maker of the stars and the moon
The author of each sun and each shower
The wonder of a heart and a hope
His design is like the secret of a flower
Who drifts in all its vibrant glory
Through the sunlight and the rainfall
Hovering beneath clinging leaves
Petals so sweet and soft, like their praise
Of a Jesus who speaks into them
Beauty, breathtaking beauty and peace

He is alive in the silence and in the voice
Of those who listen to His word
With assurance that He has been heard
By curious minds and inquisitive sentiments
Who fade into the sigh
The sound of truth being colored by faith
Belief growing louder on the heart

Who knows that He is alive
His love paints the stars in the skies
And reminds me why I'm alive
To praise Him with my heart and my soul
With every thought that I suppose
Each reflection of His love
Grows more assured that He is the One
Who gives my heart its hope
My soul its warmth and my spirit
Its abiding feelings of absolute assurance
The Holy Spirit has come down
To pour out its joy through my thoughts
Pierce my dreams with its marvels
Make me see that His very presence
Is a gift that my heart will forever treasure

Lifting my voice to be heard
By the mountains
And the moon and the stars
I praise my Jesus with my heart
And my hope and my prayer
For a love that lives eternally
Possessing me with its pure serenity
The unfolding of a melody
Brought to life by His wisdom
His light and love and gift of escape
From the darkness that doesn't hesitate
To thrust its elusive odium
Through the spirit who needs only believe
Jesus is the One who will bring
Absolute assurance, real peace, belief
So that we are saved from the thief
Who comes to destroy all our dreams

Just believe and be saved from the darkness
Which never lifts its ruin from your faith
Just believe and don't be deceived

Jesus is the only way to find peace
Jesus is the only way to know grace
That assures your heart you've been saved!

God's Child

He knows about my very worst sins
He sees my heart—my wretchedness
He knows the depths of my spirit
He sees the darkness within me
And, still, He gives me a second chance
When I can't even understand His grace

He whispers hope into my heart
He sings of light, love and more
He knows my weakness and my thoughts
He brings me a sweetness and joy
And, still, He never forsakes my soul
When I can't comprehend His kindness

He knows about the feelings that destroy
Feelings of doubt, disillusion and sorrow
He colors my dreams in cheery belief
Awakens my heart to the sincere promises
Of a Father who loves unconditionally
A God who is filled with absolute peace

He shines His sun down on my soul
He pierces my heart with His unchanging love
He guides me through shadows of despair
He reminds me that I have His strength
To encourage and bolster me during worries
Reinforce my praise of His unending mercy

He lifts me from the darkness of my pain
He inspires me to believe when I think I can't
He urges me to just let go of my dismay
He nurtures me with a love that is alive
A love so beautiful it delights and enlightens
Reminding me that I am someone He stirs

He moves my heart and soul to believe
He rouses my faith with His unending peace
He motivates my smile and my laughter
He rains down His love so that I catch His
Wonderful creativity and insight into hope
With Him, there is no doubt or dissuasion

He favors me with blessings that are so warm
He lifts my painful depression and discouragement
He promises me that His love will last forever
He guarantees His redemption is my salvation
I will always feel like I am someone worthwhile
Because of Him, I know that I am God's child

I Yearn to Know Him

I yearn to know Him
Better than I can explain
Assuring my heart and soul
Of love that is filled with hope
Love that is always in control
Of my words, my thoughts
Every part of my heart

I yearn to show Him
Just how much I love Him
How deeply I need to express
The wonder of His grace
The music pouring from His
Warm and welcome arms
The feelings that I know
Glow brighter than the sun
Raining faith into my soul
Filling me with insight, light
That brightens my entire life

I yearn to grow in Him
With beautiful dreams so alive
They fulfill all my heart's thirsts
For a drink of something soothing
Comfort that keeps me assured
That His love is always inside me
Thriving, inspiring, guiding me
Toward a better way, a new day
The opportunity to always say
He is light—He is love
He is the grace that portrays
All the beauty and wonder
Of a love that is always kind
A love that is full and alive
A love that will forever survive

I yearn to bestow on Him
The brilliance of joy He stirs
The creativity He inspires
The motivation He awakens
The vision of hope and faith
The revelation of His grace
Flowing through my veins
As His redeeming blood floods
Over my soul, cleansing me
Of the sin that lives within
Where I need Him to show me
The way toward love that glows
On my heart, soul and life
Love that is forever vibrant

I yearn to shadow Him through life
Building my faith around His sparkle
My hope around His vivacity, His wonder
My love around His promises to me
Promises to never leave me nor forsake me
To always be available, a friend until the end
Never letting me down—always abounding
With unconditional love—love that I can believe in

> *Let your conversation be without covetousness; and be content with such things as ye have: for he hath said, I will never leave thee, nor forsake thee.*
> —Hebrews 13:5

Shine Down Your Love

Shine down Your light
From your home in the sky
Rain down Your love
From the heart who gives
More than a home
More than a heart
More precious hope than
My mind can comprehend
More faith and grace than
My mind can appreciate
More inspiration than my life
Can expect to honor

Shine down Your glory
Toward the spirit inside me
Rain down Your kindness
From the spirit that guides me
Remind me that your love
Is always there, a living light
Showering me with joy, peace
And all the love I'll ever need

Shine down Your wonders
Filled with gladness and light
As I adore Your miraculous presence
Here with me, showing me the way
Leading me to the right paths
Steering me toward the honest things
The honorable and peaceful
The sensations of trust and bliss
Emptying me of worry and dread
Reassuring me that I have all I need
To reach toward my goals, my dreams
With expectation and motivation

Confidence that I have the strength
The power of One who lives inside me
Filling me up with His competence and skill
His ability to make every dream a reality

Shine down Your light of love
Breathe passion into my heart and soul
Wake up my imagination and hope
With Your wisdom and ambition, Your
Amazing vision which will assure me
That this desire within me is alive
Like a fire, a thought, a reverie
Filling me up with purest prudence
Feelings of insight, understanding
A penetrating hunger which hints at
The knowledge of a hope being fulfilled
A faith being proven—a light being stilled
By the blessed Creator, the life
Who colors my whole world in splendor
Assures my whole life of a awe
Which reminds me that love is the light
Which guides and inspires my life

Shine down Your wisdom and strength
Let me see Your glory, Your power pouring
Out a grace that penetrates my faith
And promises me that I always know the way
Toward the Savior—the light who I praise
Because He is the One who makes a way
Where there was no way and no appeal
He is the light that whispers His mercy
Into my heart and my life, through my prayers
Filling me up with a beautiful, warming Son
Who knows the way to lead me is with His love!

Redeeming Love

I searched for the whisper of love
Coloring my hopes in kindness and light
Expressions of joy raining down from above
Precious feelings to cheer the darkest night
Reminding hearts of a love story they can write

I wanted to feel the glorious inspirations
Found in the heart who feels love's sweetness
Lingering grace with wonderous sensations
Filling my life with assurance and completeness
Amazing my spirit with its absolute discreetness

I yearned for the miracle that would bring me
The promise of an affection that never suspected
Vowing to give my heart gentleness so it would agree
The value of this tenderness with whom I'm connected
Bringing adoration that is alive and is totally perfected

I hoped that I would be blessed with this devotion
That comes to those who listen to the sound of the heart
Who reminds them that real love is more than emotion
It comes from the spirit whose hope will never depart
The one who knows that this impression will never fall apart

I sought a love that would always be alive, forever
Giving from the spirit, with sincerity and expectation
That everything in life will be brighter and never
Allow the pains and worries of life to end the elation
That came to life when I finally found sweet salvation

When I Pray

I pray to the One who knows me
Even better than I know myself
The King of Kings, the Peace, the gift
From a God who understands
I am imperfect but I am still His
And I need to feel His grace
Pouring comfort through my praise

I pray to the God in heaven
Who allows me to reach my goals
With assurance that I can make it
Because He always shares with me
Love that is beautiful and alive
Helping me to always survive
The tests of doubt and confusion
The worry, pain and disillusionment

I pray to the Wonder of Wonders
The One who gave up His life
So that I might know Him and discover
The way toward a heaven where I know
He awaits me, ready to bestow
Love that I can only dream of, so gentle
That its touch is far above my dreams
So very perfect that I know anything
That comes to me will be glorious
Alive with joy and hope and peace
Comfort that reminds me to believe
That God is never weary of my needs
And He will always be there, eternally

The Rudiments of Wings

Holy prayers
Shine light from above
Sacred grace
Falling soft on the heart
As angels fly
Wings breathing satisfaction

Heavenly promises
Sing silent and warm
Throbbing revelations
Coloring the spirit
In a vision of sweet joy
As angels smile
Wings beckoning, fearless

Beautiful feelings
Bound in faith
Pour over the spirit
Who knows the way
To glory, love
Is found in the One
Who angels
Call upon with dreams
Wings vibrating, peace

Like a stardust wonder
Faith silences
The darkness, the thunder
Gentling wild hearts
With praise
Longings from voices
Courageous,
Sensing the compassion
Breathless angels

Phenomenon
Wings bent in prayer

Wings, powerful and sure
Vow to God
Then take up the flight
To worship in truth
Adoration and devotion
With respect
That will last forever
Angels admire
With wings of reverence

My God, My F O R E V E R

In the flowers and the trees
I see His light surrounding me

In the whisper of a morning breeze
I feel His hope bringing me to my knees

In the breath of a warm, Spring shower
I consider His wonder that brings such power

In the silence of a peaceful night sky
I know His joy will never say good-bye

In the music of sweet Autumn leaves falling
I realize His precious love is forever calling

In the beauty of soft, breathless snowflakes
I understand His grace heals even heartbreaks

In the sweetness of a Summer sunset
I appreciate His kindness I won't forget

In the laughter of the brilliant sunshine
I recognize His peace filling His design

In the colors of the morning prayer
I discern His grace which is always aware

In the blessings that come to life
I grasp His restoration from all strife

In the glory of nature's lovely song
I perceive His power so very strong

In the life that He has blessed me thru
I can tell His love just grew and grew

In my heart and soul, where I always know
I touch His spirit with prayers all aglow

In my best and worst, whatever occurs
I sense His presence with me through the years

In this life, I carry my hopes and dreams to Him
I know that He will love me through every whim

In everything that comes, good or bad or whatsoever
I experience assurance with Him, my God, my forever!

Vein of Prayer

Pouring out my heart
On the empty page
With a silent prayer
And a whisper of faith
Pen birthing grace
Inspired by His face

Raining down love
He shines from up above
Freeing my heart
From fear that taunts
From tears that haunt
From darkness and dread
He silences the screams
Of a heart bleeding
Through veins of prayer

Filling my mind with joy
That comes from finally knowing
His love is the only answer
To my prayers for peace and wisdom
Prayers for light and love
That leaves me with so much warmth
Hope that lingers on and on
Glowing in the shadows
Beckoning to my heart's thanksgiving
Blessing me with inspiration
Freeing my imagination
So that His love is my eternal wealth!

Thankful for Grace

Grace called my name in a breath
Of light falling softly, gentle
Across my spirit, through my heart
Beckoning my soul to listen
With a whisper, I became His
The child who would always know
He is there, alive inside where I hope
A light of love, light of joy, light of life
Rains down a sense of new beginnings
Creating tenderness in prayers
For those who need to believe in Him
The One who gives us all the hope
We need to continue on, keep going
Never quitting or giving up on our dreams
With Him, there is the assurance
Of a love that lives and breathes,
Guides me through the heartaches
Through the darkest storms that come
On toward the joy and peace of knowing
God is alive and He is still on the throne
In control of it all despite all the fear
That seems to come to the heart
Who fails to listen to His direction
And understand the love in His protection

Grace like this is alive, a living thing
Coloring my soul in hues of kindness, gentleness
Faith in the Savior who lived and breathed
But died on a tree so that I could finally be
Saved from my sin and redeemed by His blood
Filled with unending peace, a sense of thanks
For the joy that brings my heart hope
My feelings a sense of assurance, pure love
That comes from knowing this Jesus

Who brought me through the darkness
Who is there to reveal every good thing that comes
Every joy and hope, every peace and love
All the wonders of living under His grace
With the sweetest feeling of prayer, praise
For the One who guides me through the worst
And fills my heart with a generosity, a hope
For the love that comes alive inside my soul
Because I know the One who brought me through
The shadows of pain, sorrow and shame
The discouragement of a place where I had to face
All the bad and the sad, the lonely and lost
The heartless place of despair where I yearned
To open up my heart, to share, to show the love
That is poured out on the soul who knows
That His only Son, the lover of my soul
Is alive and well, living inside my heart
Bringing peace and hope, promises of much more
Love than I could ever hope to know
Love that is filling my entire life with wonder

Grace brings to life the inspiration, the warmth
Of a life that knows God is alive, on the throne,
Giving His perfect love to the ones who know
He is the answer to every question, every prayer
Every request for a new and better way to thank Him!

He BLESSED Me

He blessed me with hope
When my feelings told me
I didn't have a chance
That misery was my condition
And I'd never see the wisdom
Of giving from my heart
A part of my kindness and grace
Knowing that my prayers
Would somehow bring my faith
All the assurance that I needed
To just let go and keep believing

He blessed me with courage
When I wasn't feeling very strong
Almost like I was completely wrong
And didn't have a leg to stand on
Because my heart was weak, so weak
It felt like I couldn't breath
Like something inside me stirred
In the darkness and dread, the fear
That awakened my yearning for
A sense of serenity and strength
That comes from giving in to Him
Leaning on His power and love
Without ever doubting His grace
He is the One who can lift me
From the darkest of the shadows
The dimness of the bluest tear
The night of that piercing dread
The feelings that bring terror
Beckoning me to nightmares
And coloring my hopes in blackness

He blessed me with fulfillment
Serenity amid the chaotic
Joy when all seems lost
Inspiration when life is hard
A melody when I don't have a song
Light when the night is so bleak
Beauty when gloom seeks me

He blessed me with a everlasting love
The kind that brings true joy
And wisdom from His home above
The kind that grows truth and kindness
Laughter amid the haunting despair
Gentleness when all else seems futile
Friendship that will never fail
The miracle of a faith that is alive
Living in the soul, coloring all the life
In sincerity and wonder, elation
That comes from knowing
This God of the bible, the same One
My whole life and hope is based on
Will someday welcome me home
To the heaven where He is waiting for me!

He blessed me with His Son
And His love lingers on and on

The Night Sky

High above my thoughts and form
There breathes a light so beautiful
It strongly resembles a giant pearl
Hung in the night by threads of hope
Whispering effortlessly across the sky
Echoing pleasure through the heart
It reflects all the kindness I have sought
As my soul prays for a touch from God
God who knows that I need His love
Much more than I need this world
Or anything that man might conceive of

Piercing the darkness with intense twinkling
There lives small reflections of love's gentleness
Dangling on hidden gossamers shadowed by night
Tossed on the sky like small enchanting flickers
Flames of inspiration stabbing the black nocturnal
Reaching beyond the darkness toward the birth
Of a passionate sun who needs only to come undone
With its vibrant passion, its roar of creativeness
Stars shimmering down to join the moon in worship

I linger in the obscurity of a night sky
Reflecting on the emotions, both powerful
And stirring—brought to the surface
Of a darkness who remembers only to feel
The ebb and flow of a sensitivity colored
In hues of sincerity, shadowed by tears
Who seems to pray for only one more glimpse of
The kindness bestowed on an empty planet
By the loving Father who created this tenderness
Moon and stars who mirror the sun's hope
And shine through the evening, soothing and gentle
Praising a Creator who gave them their time

To whisper their charms on the skies, the atmosphere
Through the world who knows only that God is alive
Breathing His music through the night skies.

The Savior of the World

There are times when I seek Him
With all my heart and soul
But just can't seem to see Him
In the life where I know
He is keeping me from harm
Kissing me with light
Whispering peace into my thoughts
And coloring me in hues of hope

There are moments when I yearn
To touch His heart with my own
But I just can't find Him
In my life, where I see only strife

I yearn for Him and His blessing
The gentleness of His affection
I reach out for His hand
Expecting His grace and mercy
To pour over me like a river
Even though I know I'm so unworthy
And can't possibly give Him
All the praise and honor He deserves

There are days when I just can't pray
And the trust I feel is a trust
That questions all His answers and reactions
I want to be the child that He can know
Will always love Him with a heart of hope
And give to Him the admiration that I should
With worship that reminds Him
I am His child, His chosen one, His beloved
I am someone who loves Him wholeheartedly
With a love that is kind, warm and good

I long for His permission to reach out
With a knowing that He will be there
If I should ever need His help, His protection
His kindness, wonder and affection
He will be there through the good and bad
Amid the happy as well as the sad
He will teach me to always listen to His voice
Knowing in my heart that I have a choice
I can worship Him and share in His love
Or relinquish my joy to this tired old world

I choose the Father who gave me His Son
So that I might become a child of the One
Who poured out blessings beyond my dreams
Blessings of faith and hope, blessings
Of love that are more beautiful than anything

He is the answer to my every need
He reassures and inspires me
To reach for the best and always attest
To the fact that He is so amazing
And that, my friend, is why I praise Him!

Praise God today and eternally believe
He will touch your heart with a sense of peace
Praise God and know that He will always be
There by your side—exalting your faith
Let Him be your guide and always know
Wherever you go—You will find grace
Just believe and you can know He is
Alive inside your soul—a light to guide
Reflecting all the good that abides

Praise God—forever and always
For He is above reproach
He is the kindness
That you will delight in!

Praise God and know in your soul
He is the Savior of the world!

In the Moments

There are moments
When I don't know how to pray
There are moments
When I don't know what to say
There are moments
When doubt and worry get in the way
There are moments
When I can't see the light of day

These quiet moments
When silence echoes on my soul
These dark moments
When despair forms a sinkhole
These pensive moments
When worries seem to control
These sober moments
When love is the only thing to console

That is the time—the moments
When I feel like my heart is greedy
For the love and joy and peace
That colors me in hues that are so needy
For the light that falls on my spirit
Pulling me through all those unready
Things that bring my heart strife
Like a garden who is flourishing but weedy

These are the moments when I cry
Because my heart is so filled with doubt
That I linger in the temptation to strive
For the comfort and relief poured out
From a heavenly Father who knows my sorrow
And fills me with inspiration all about
The wonder and beauty of His love and peace

The light that lingers inside with a shout
Of joy that comes from finally knowing
God is alive, pouring out rain across the drought

These moments come to remind me why
I have a peace amid the worry I can't deny
That is the reason why I always try
To hold onto the One who always will supply
Hope, faith and unending grace that will dry
All of my tears with a love on which I can rely

Silent Prayers

Silent prayers reflect my most intimate dreams
Inspirations so brilliant they color me in light
Laughing with joy like liquid flows in streams

Gentle whispers breathe hope into the schemes
Hearts blessed by a love so great it will excite
Silent prayers reflect my most intimate dreams

Kindness falls blindly through the lost screams
Passions so penetrating they crave sweet insight
Laughing with joy like liquid flows in streams

Warming spirits with a grace like soft moonbeams
Beautiful and bright, inspiring wisdom to recite
Silent prayers reflect my most intimate dreams

Melodies live in the pages of such loving themes
Surrounded by wonders of tenderness in twilight
Laughing with joy like liquid flows in streams

His mercies reign forever—His compassion redeems
The angels shine around us, allowing us to unite
Silent prayers reflect my most intimate dreams
Laughing with joy like liquid flows in streams

I'm Not a Very Good Christian

I'm not a very good Christian
There are days when I don't do it right
I think of all of my worries and sorrows
Without giving God the glory and praise
I let circumstances bring me down in the muck
Of depression, darkness and despair
I feel like I've given every part of my heart
To something other than the One
Who gave me my heart and soul to begin with
And forgave me for all the selfishness and sin

I'm not a very good Christian
There are times when I let life break through
The joy and inspiration He brings me
With His precious love, His wisdom and grace
The feelings that remind me I'm blessed
Beyond any dreams I might have had
More than I can believe when I consider
All the promises He's guaranteed with His hope
For a time when I will spend eternity
In the light of His love, His warmth, His glory

I'm not a very good Christian
There seems to be so much of His word
That simply goes unheard—I just don't listen
And He never fails to give me the opportunity to
Heed His kindness and mercy, His wonder
The beauty that falls from His mercifulness
When I fail to hear with my heart
He sometimes gestures to me with a thought
A reminder that I must let go of control
And allow Him to color my world in His love

I'm not a very good Christian
My faith isn't always a shining example of love
My hopes are sometimes filled with selfishness
And my love isn't always stirred as it should be
I'm not always filled with generosity or kindness
My soul isn't always armed with goodness
I don't always treasure the joy of someone else
In the same way I cherish my own godsends

No—I'm not a very good Christian
But, a Christian I am all the same
When He gave me the chance to become His child
He didn't say I had to be perfect or whole
I'm not the finished product by any means
But I am His and through faith, by His grace
I have been saved and delivered from sin
And, I know that He loves me unconditionally
With a love that never ends—It is eternal
And, even though I'm not a very good Christian
He made me see that to Him, I am worthy

A Humble Heart

She was always meek and mild
Mannered . . . like a smile
Filling up the room with pleasure
Gentle faith and quiet joy
Inspiring hearts to listen to the One
Who speaks in the stillness
And lights up the entire heart
With beauty so alive
It pours hope through the soul
Silences the busyness
Colors the air in hues of brilliance

She whispered to the mind
Who echoed her delight
In creativity and revelation
Music in notes of appreciation
Kindness falls from her pores
As she faces the weary
Thoughts of despair, in prayer
For the grace to face
Every moment of bleakness
With mercy and thanksgiving

She calms the stormy emotions
Tones of warmth on the surface
Of cool, clear thoughts
A wandering imagination, expectations
Living amid the stardust hopes
Enchanting passions
With knees bent to pray
Leaving darkness and dread
Falling in the shadows
Penetrating the intimate rays
Of laughing sunshine

She delights in the truth
Welcomes the music of courage
Strengthening the composure
Of the heart who knows her
Sees her goodness, her godliness
Beauty mesmerizing, bright
Desires playing with the edges
With a caress, embracing
The details of her love, her praise
Her abundant, believing, faith

She is the hint of splendor
Amid the dead leaves in Autumn
Falling gracefully, lightly
Over a bed of wildflowers in vibrant
Rich blushes of lilac and rose
Healing hearts with tangerine dreams
And crimson ideas, themes
Born on the moments of Spring
Lifting away the dry, arid sarcasm
Of a Summer drought, the way
Some other woman might weep
When the Fall gives way to white peaks

Her heart and soul make me know
Love like this is beyond words
It is light and laughter and living
It is grace and glory and giving
It is the answer to a solemn prayer
It lifts the melancholy whispers
Of glossy tears, fears that come
From the heart who listens to worry
And never knows the certainty
God is there forever, eternally
Giving His love to those who know
He is the One we're living for!

Glorious Savior

Glorious Savior
My heart is in Your hands
Lead me and guide me
Show me all of Your plans

Jesus, my redeemer,
Lover of my spirit and soul
Wonder of all wonders
Comforter who does console

Light of the heavens
Peace beyond any other
Fill my life with singing
Knowing You're my brother

Whisper of inspiration
Flowing soft against my mind
Leaving Your gentle spirit
To assure me of what I'll find

Precious deliverer, Holy One
Lift my heart so that I can see
All the joy that You've brought
When I choose to bend my knee

Heaven's special gift of hope
Send your breath of cherished love
Covering me with such sensations
That could only come from up above

Silence every worry and angst
Relieve all my sorrow and my fears
Color me in a tender embrace
Wipe away all my lingering tears

Dear Father of all creation
Lift the darkness with your light
Send angels of joy and faith
To pour out kindness on the night

Jesus, I hope You know
My love for You just grows and grows
It is bigger than the biggest ocean
More bright and beautiful than a rose

Jesus, dear loving friend
Know that Your glory has filled me
With a grace that lights my soul
Delivering me so that I can be free

Jesus, I love you—eternally
You are the answer to bring sincerity
Poured out on hearts who believe
Your unending light shines with charity

You are the answer to my every prayer
You make every dream come true
With Your love, You fill me with my share
Of joy and hope, faith to see me through!

Wonder of Wonders

This is the wonder of wonders—That God blessed us with such a confession of His absolute glory!
—BY POET

Dazzling dewdrops
Slide slowly, brilliant, vibrant
Across the petals so wise
With singsong beauty
In hues of praise, sweet grace
Reflections of joy
Penetrating dreams, awake

Collections of flowers
Buds stirred to life
By the melody of birds
Tunes, softly sung
Rising to the laughing sun
Who welcomes the morning
With lemon yellow tones
Echoing sparkling rays
Across the edge of an azure sky

Deep shadows, forlorn
Whisper comfort to the moon
Shimmering in its night
Beckoning to the twinkling stars
Signaling the silent ease
Of a bright kindness
Overflowing the glow in the sky
Reminding hearts just why
There is heaven in sight

Wonders of the moment
Squirrels scampering to and fro
Laughing at the oak
Who never seems more bold
As its branches grasp
Turning with the winds
Awakening a sense of tenderness
In the reverberating gales
Thrilling the air with promises
Of the lone love story

Will this flicker of hope
Drown out the darkness
Returning courage
Jubilant strength and mercy
To the soul who knows
His touch is on the whole
Embracing the world
In an aching love that longs
To be shown, exposed
By the sensitivity of nature
It's insight into the spirit
It's prudence and sagacity
It's understanding and amazing
Way of giving every heart
Pleasure that is like a smile
Soft, easy, filling the face
With rays of sunshine intimacy

Reach for the Peace

Unable to make it on my own
I reach for His hand
My light, my hope—the answer
To the prayers I have prayed
The ones where I tell Him
To come close and be my aide

When I can't make it
Not even another day
I call out to my Savior
And He answers my call
With kindness and mercy
Grace that prevents me
From falling without Him
The One who always
Makes a way to find peace
A way to unearth the joy
A way to restore all I've lost
In the battle toward the cross

Not even my best friend
Can help me when I'm down
At my worst, without a chance
I feel like I'm buried in the sand
Reaching toward the dream
Without possibility of coming out
Of the darkness, the storm
That surrounds me with its fury
Its pain, doubt and disillusionment

There are moments in my life
When I hesitate to believe
Can I walk away from this strife?
It is so furious and fights within me

For the precious peace of mind
That I need to finally be free
Of the dread that haunts my soul
With despair, fear—I am desperate
To find a way out of these shadows
Of pain, regret, shame—anguish

Never let the enemy make you believe
Jesus won't come to help you
When you're in need, He will be there
Lighting the path toward joy
Coloring the heart in wonder and grace
Filling the soul with a love that gives
Hope and peace—a whisper of gentleness
The assurance that your needs
Will be comforted, soothed by the belief
That you have in this Jesus
Who is everything, everywhere, every
Anticipation for answered prayers

Yes, there comes the blackness
When we fall beneath the silhouettes
Of gloom and despair, fear that defeats
But there is such a wonderful truth
That comes alive on the heart who chooses
To believe in Jesus and His amazing blood
Which covers the sins of every heart
With the assurance that salvation is won
By believing in a Savior who died
Rose from the grave and went home
To sit on the right hand of the Father
Who will bring us all home to heaven
After this troublesome life is done!

Just believe and find the peace
That only Jesus is capable of bringing!

With Love Always

He listened to my worries and fears
Taught me about love and joy
Inspired me to listen to the heart
Find the wonder in a smile
Lift up my brother so he could see
The light of our Father
Burning from that long ago tree

He left me feeling like I was worthwhile
Even thought I didn't know why
He colored my hopes in vibrant feelings
Placed kindness on my soul, a sense
Of what it means to let go and let God
Finding the answers in the word
Where He left me so many tender verses

He poured out His wisdom upon my spirit
Sent His angels to guide me
Reminding me that I can find the strength
Even when I'm feeling so alone, so weak
He encouraged me to give all I can
Liberally, generously, without any demands
With a heart who knows what it is
To whisper I love you from gentle tears

He graced my dreams with a burning passion
Rained down His blessings on my soul
Filling me with sensations of warmth and gladness
Stirring the hopes that bind my reveries
With faith that keeps believing
In spite if the worries and fears, the anxieties
That keep me filled with needless doubt
Damaging even the shadows of promise, prospects
With discouragement, despair and darkness

He lifted my heart from the filthy ruins
Of loss and loneliness, disbelief, confusion
Helping me to remember that I can do
Anything that I believe in my heart
He has for me—be it big or small, obvious
Or like a invisible detail, a thought
Love born of compassion, consideration, care
For the one who knows that God
Is alive and well, living on the inside of those
Who pray for His guidance and direction

He showered me with a love that is beyond compare
It lights up the darkest night with joy
Arouses the broken heart to hear, to admire
All the music that comes alive on the soul
Who knows that His love comes to give us so much more
Than we have ever had before, more joy
More peace, more tenderness, more faith, more
Of everything that is good and of God
He heals and fills the soul with love that is beyond
Any hopes or dreams, beyond the thinking
It is rich in sensations of faith and gives unconditionally

He made a way where no way had been before
Let me know that I am His child
The apple of His eye, blessed like no one else
With a blessing that comes to life
On my heart and soul, in the pores of my smile
He prompts me to always know
His love is an open door, an opportunity
For discovering the warmth of a home in heaven
A place I'll be given to keep forevermore
As I praise the One who gave me so much love
Love that I will always be sure of
Love that is alive inside my soul, opening minds
Opening hearts and filling us all with
The One who knows we were bought and paid for
By His light, His love, His life

He is the answer to every need
Just pray and say
Jesus, make a way where there has been no way
And listen to His reply with faith
Belief that He is all we ever really need
With Him, we are complete
In Him, we find hope, faith and love
He is the answer to everything
And He is the One I'll love eternally!

My Father

Dear Father of love that frees
Love that colors the heart in hues
Of wonderful blessings, inspirations
So brilliant they shine through
The spirit with tenderness, affection
Praise of the One who brought me
Through the storms, across the seas
Past the worry, fear and anxiety

Dear Father of my heart and hope
Still the darkness that works to
Frighten me into a place of despair
Fill me with your light, your joy
The miracle of a peace so perfect
It pours out kindness through me
Shining gentleness over my thoughts
Reminding me why I can always hope
Through the sorrows and tears
There is always His love living here
Within my soul when I can surely know
Love this alive is bound to survive
The tests of time, the haunting, the strife

Dear Father of my spirit, send your light
To breathe tenderness through my thoughts
Lift my dreams so that I can continue to hope
Whisper prayers from my yearnings and dreams
Reminding me that love is always here with me
Beckoning to my spirit to believe in His truth
The music of a heart who knows this is real
This beautiful faith that awaits the day
When I can silence every worry with a smile
Revealing the glory God sends to His child

Dear Father of my insight and imagination
Reflect all the glory that You still send
Despite my doubts and fears, my worries
You remind me that I can do anything
With You there beside me, guiding me
Inspiring me to be the person You meant
For me to be from the beginning, even
When I was still sinning and still in need of
Salvation from the darkness that haunted
My hopes and dreams, my ideas and beliefs
Even when I didn't know the joy of this light
You knew that I was Yours and that I would arise
From the shadows that darkened my faith
And left me feeling like I was such a disgrace

Dear Father of my life—my hope and insight
Please don't ever leave me without your grace
Raining down joy across my heart and soul
Filling me with kindness, serenity and wonder
Feelings that were inspired by the love You
Poured out over my life, freeing me from strife!

Dear Father, God, my Savior and Creator –
Thank You for Your salvation—You are amazing!

Living Proof

His spirit caresses my heart
Filling me with the joy that is alive
Whispering through the silence
Of beauty and inspiration
Love that penetrates the soul
With the wonder of His brilliance
Streaming through the heavens
Light that reflects so many blessings
Poured out on the one who listens
To faith that believes without question
Believing in the One who came here
To give us a second chance,
A new beginning, salvation of a soul
Who knows the miracle of His grace
Falling soft upon the heart who thinks
He is more amazing than the seas
More worthy of praising than any hope
More hopeful than any vision I know

With Him, there is only the prayer
Of a heart who knows He is always there
Always aware of everything that comes
Every worry, fear—every tear that haunts
The worst there is will surely be consoled
By the power of His spirit sent here to give
Complete assurance, comfort, grace
Guarantee that He is alive on the inside
Where His spirit whispers wonder and love
Proof that He came down to us from above!

You Are the Answer

Dear Lord, I ask
Do your will through me
Let me shine your light, your love
Your kindness, hope and faith from above
Let me show others the wonders
You've shown me through my heart
Let me give back a small portion of the joy
You've left inside—spilling out into my life
Reminding me that Your love is like sunshine
Always alive, always shining, always warm—pouring
Out beauty, peace and grace—a silent whisper
Of music that will erase every worry or fear, all my tears

Dear Lord, I ask
Do with me what you will
Fill my life with kind words and purpose
Make me into someone who is worthy
Show me how to give generously, liberally
Free my heart to be available to give away
Some of the wonder you've planted inside
A bit of the gentleness, the smiles, the delight
The inspiration, imagination and insight
All the contentment that comes from knowing
You are the answer and with You I have assurance
That this life I'm living is the one you have blessed
With the miracle of peace, promise and patience
The joy of a life that is guided by sweet faith
And sanctified by the One who made me to believe
This is the time to reach out with complete surety
That God brings so much love out of every circumstance
Filling my heart with the grace to live as He says
With a sincere appreciation for the blessings He shares

Dear Lord, I ask You
Please do your will through me
Fill me to overflowing with your word
So that I always know the difference in good and bad
So that I grow stronger through the weakness I've seen
So that I can see YOU in every part of my heart and soul
So that I know what it is to give from the depths of my spirit
So that I reflect on the wisdom You give so generously
So that I feel the way that You intended for me to feel
So that I let You know when I need You to heal my hurts
So that I allow You the free reign in every part of my life
So that I realize the importance of praying about everything

Dear Lord, I ask You
Please have your will, your way, in my life and heart
Fill me with understanding and hope,
Faith that never lets me doubt
The wonder of a promise who answers my worries
With assurance that I will find peace and assurance
The chance to give back to You, Lord
A bit of the love that You have bestowed

Dear Lord, I ask You
Please guide me toward the right path
Let me feel You with me in my spirit
Where I know that You will give me
The love that it takes to bring hope and grace
To someone else, someone who needs to know
That You are the one who is guiding my soul
You are the One who answers all my questions
You are the light that lingers in my silence
You are the music to free me from darkness
You are the One who makes me feel like I'm alive
Even when I'm sad, depressed or lacking faith
To find the inspiration to reach out with thanks

You, dear Lord, are the answer to my every prayer
You are the love that I carry everywhere!

Thank You, Lord . . . for Your embrace
Your gentleness and grace
For the love on your face
When I reach out to You with praise!

Thank You, Lord—I love YOU today and every day!

A Heavenly Home

Laughter falls over my thoughts
Pouring joy into me like hope lingering
On stardust nights, brilliant as a smile
Hungry like my heart as it grows closer
To the Son, the Light, the One
Who I base my life, my hope, upon

Jesus came down to shine His light
Across the lives who know
He is the hope we've been praying for
The grace we've been waiting for
The second chance for love that abides
In the heart He fills with His glorious light

Joy is rained down like dewdrop dreams
Emptying the heaven's endless glory
So that we can feel the beauty and peace
The whisper of a tenderness, a caress
Lifting all the worry and fear, piercing
The darkest shadows with His magnificence
His brilliant rays of wonder and inspiration
Feelings that flow through our hearts
Fill us up with a sense of acceptance
The miracle of a grace that unfolds into
The heart who knows that His love
Is the answer to every prayer, every need
The answer that supplies and agrees
Love like this fulfills our heart's demands
While assuring our souls that we have
Everything we need to reach heaven's home

The Notebook

Silent tears flowing
Listening to the lost moments
Songs so warm echoing
Through my mind, designed
To breathe memories
Poured out over my yearnings

Blushing dreams whisper
Vibrant as sunlight and stardust
Caressing my spirit
With lavender wishes, whimsical
Laughter growing hues
Of wonder and mystery

Praying comfort, kindness, blessings
Over hearts who scream
In dark shadows of fear and dread
Asking the One who made us
For a peace that is alive
With second chances to survive

Soft praises, dressed in purity
Linger on the lips of inspiration
Fulfilling yearnings for tenderness
Walking gently in the imagination
Reflecting all the hope, peace and love
Wound through hearts resonating joy

In the notebook of needs
There in my mind
Lives the promise of His grace
Given in assurance
That His blood will cover sins
So my weary heart can begin again

Nothing but Blue Skies

Rain kissed my thoughts with a song
Coloring my dreams in laughter and hope
Vibrant whispers of joy so kind, light
Falling soft across each poem I write

Silent prayers, thanking the Creator
Praising Him with every sigh, each breath
Flowing rivers of inspiration, imagination
Insight into the wonders of His grace

Serenity coloring hearts in the amazement
Of tenderness alive with sincerity, kindness
Dreams felt on the shadows of His wisdom
Pouring out sensations and sunshine cravings

Feathery smiles from a glory beyond words
Touches the spirit, establishing His compassion
Brilliant smiles of sunshine embraces hugging
Hearts with a million stardust moments

The morning sighed under the weight of His love
Evening winds soothed the night with stars
Reflecting on the silence in wonders alive
And the sky had never been so vibrant a hue of blue

Autumn Years

I've come to my autumn years
While my heart falls silent
Trembling with its gentle tears
Reflecting on the former things
Some hopes and other fears

I've come to my ending days
When my soul yearns for light
Shining tenderness who prays
For comfort of the worrier
Needing healing of anxious ways

I've come to my lost, faded dreams
When breathless smiles reach out
Caressing me with joys it seems
Alive and yearning in hues of grace
Ringing with kindly, rosy themes

I've come to my darkest dismay
Whispering fright in nightmares
Weakening one who will portray
All the sweetness of joyful prayers
Praise of the One who I'll not betray

I've come to my finishing of the race
Reflecting on the gentleness of thanks
Raining down love that can't replace
The music in the soul, the wonderous hope
Of an affection I'll never be able to erase

I've come to my conclusion, lastly
Awakening life in the heart and soul
Coloring feelings in hues so vastly
They stir up promises of the end
When love burns so alive, steadfastly

I've come to my close of my lifetime
Where my spirit reflects on insights
Basking in joys that lived in old time
When my heart was more familiar
With the presence of famous springtime

Whether I let the past embrace me
With its splendors, it's exaltations
Or I finally let go and simply agree
The time has come to turn my heart
Toward God where I'll be set free

I'll let go and let God take my soul
Up to the heavens where I'll give Him
All my praise, all my spirit to console
With the knowledge that I'm living
With the One who made my heart whole

Lord, Please Help Me

Lord, please help me
I feel like the walls are closing in
Everywhere I look
There is sorrow, darkness and sin

Lord, please help me
I'm walking through a strange land
There is so much pain
And it sometimes feels like more than I can stand

Lord, please help me
I let the worries and sadness into my life
When I yearn for joy
I only feel the discouragement of strife

Lord, please help me
I'm never quite sure I'm on the right track
There is such a feeling of loneliness
My adversary is always there to attack

Lord, please help me
I long to know what it means to hope
There is so much dread
Filling my mind without any way to cope

Lord, please help me
Send down your love to fill my soul
Hear the prayers that I pray
Answer me with serenity to console

Lord, please help me
Lift up my heart with your grace
Free me from this burden
Of fear—lighten my load with your embrace

Lord, please help me
Don't ever turn me away
You're the One
Who makes me able to say . . .

Lord, please help me
I know you're always there
And I can always know
Your love is forever aware

Lord, please help me
Without a doubt, you're the One
Who brightens my life
With love that shines like the Son

You're the answer to my every prayer
The reason that I lift my heart from despair
Crying out to You because I always know
You're there for me and You truly do care

Lord, thank you
For always being there
A light of hope, faith and love
Sent down from my home above!

My Collections

I collect smiles
From those I haven't seen in a while
They always remind me why
I feel blessed to be a part of their life
Their light, their insight and quiet
Feelings of comradery and cheer
Kindness that is so alive and so real
Love that kindles whispers of inspiration
Flowing through my mind and coloring
My imagination in joy, hope and peace
All the flavors of beautiful dreams!

I gather laughter
From the hearts and souls who share
Parts of their life and love, their wonder
The sweetness of lives so adorable,
So brilliant and warm and promising
Like a flower just opening to show the world
It's feathery joy, it's bloom of such glory
Unfading, flaming with vibrant hues
Of peace that whispers of sensational
Attraction to love, praying and praising
The One who creates every amazement!

I store up happiness
From spirits alive with the joy that comes
Alive on the lives of those who know love
Will stir feelings to breath deeply of light
Which pierces the darkness, dancing rays
Of sunny intuition which sooths the gaze with
Delicious freedom from the worry, the fear
That seems to live on broken hearts, broken
By the pain that comes from losing a friend
Losing love that would never ever end

To the past who stares back in wheezing
Wishes, lingering on the emotion who grows silent
Like a prayer being spoken by the soul
Who knows that only God can comfort and heal
With His gentle presence, His grace, His will
To give the gift of contentment to those who
He chooses to love tenderly because He truly is
A good, good Father, a friend, a serenity
So real that we can't comprehend His creativeness
Or His mystery—He is the One I believe in
With appreciation for His gift to me—His love
That is stronger than any worry, fear or tear
His love is the reason I know what it is to be redeemed
By a grace that lives in the center of love so precious
A love that is alive, the answer to survival . . .
Jesus, the help who knows all about me and loves me
With a love that is beyond my comprehension.
It is a love that gives and lives forevermore!

I collect this gift for me . . .
Inside a heart who believes in Him
The One who shines down truth in me
And gives me a second chance to be
The woman that loves unconditionally
With a love that He pours into me!

A Letter to God

Dear God of love
Send hope from above
You're the answer to a prayer
For light to smile across this heart
Whispering faith, joy and grace

Please, dear God
Shed your wonder from above
Your kind and gentle favor
Upon the soul who labors
Longing for the answer, the way
To find serenity in the day
When hurt has been the companion
And leaving a heart feeling less than
Almost like there is no answer

Please, dear God above
Rain down the sweetness of your love
Open the door to faith that abides
Breathing inspiration on the inside
Where I know you will always reside
A intimate peace that is so very alive
You shine through the spirit
Burning away the darkness and doubt
Filling me up with kindness throughout

Please, dear God, my Father
Send your grace to this place
Of sadness and worry, pain and dread
Fear that mingles with sorrow
Bringing disgrace to the heart
And crushing the spirit with thoughts
That bring destruction and despair
A shadow of the heart in pain

Feelings so humbling they never fade
But silence all the joy that might be

Dear God in heaven,
Please pour out your warmth
Freeing me to love like you do
With a love that is wise and true
A love that is like a prayer of praise
Calming the soul and soothing the faith
Of one who loves beyond their dreams
With a love that You have inspired
A love that You left inside them
There to lift, love and guide them
With hope for the promises you sent
With the scriptures, sweet tenderness

Dear God, my beautiful treasure,
The One I know as life, light and love
The answer to my every hope or doubt
The reason I can say that love is alive
And that I know what it means to shout
With a wonder of joy that comes from knowing
You are here with me, living in my soul
Singing triumphantly of joy forevermore
Joy that comes from the hope of heaven
Where You are waiting for me to enter!

Holy Spirit

I want to know you better
Your light falling over my thoughts
Piercing the quiet darkness
That shadows my feelings, my heart

I want to feel your love pour out
In the silence of a still night
Coloring my soul in dreams fulfilled
By your guiding light, your insight
The wonder of your gentle flow
Of love so wonderful it breathes
A glow reflecting upon my feelings

I want to see you reach out to me
With a hand who created the world
Silence the darkness' whispers
With kindness that captures hope
On the sunshine moments when I
Remember the love that fills me up

I want to understand your wonders
The freedoms you give to my spirit
The rise and fall of the sea's waves
The whisper of a smile so fulfilling
Like music to brighten the winds
With soft sighs and miracles who believe
You are the risen Savior, the One
Who I praise with my every word
The King who makes my life worthwhile

I want to recognize your blessings
Being rained down from the heavens
Like a nourishing shower of compassion
Stirring the flames of kindness and praise

The music of a psalm which will calm
Every worry, each doubt, all the grief
That yearns to torture me with shame
Burden my mind with a fog of blame

I want to realize how far you've brought me
From the wretchedness of a lost thought
To the joy of unending hope, a silent prayer
Spoken on the soul of this love for Him who knows
Me like no other ever could, with a knowledge of
All that is bad and all that is good, every thought
That I have you know and comprehend, like a friend
Who is alive in my heart where your love flows
With its peace and hope, its tender warmth
Love that is gracious and grateful, so very thankful
For the One who lives in my heart, forever a part
Of my dreams, my feelings, my ideas—fulfilling

Without you, my Jesus, I'm not living
With you, I breathe this sense of giving
That fills me up with your Holy Spirit

Grief That Won't Let You Go

She was grieving inside her soul
Longing for hope to open a door
She couldn't rest in her broken heart
Her spirit was melting from the flames
Of a sadness that penetrated her mind
Fell across her life like a shadow of night
Never allowing the wonder of His joy inside

She was angry, lost in the sorrow
Her heart felt faint and her life was so quiet
Without the one she loved, the one who
Was taken up to heaven, beyond her grasp
Without this little one, her faith felt flat
As if she couldn't chance the thought
Of feeling better or letting go of the hurt

She was growing more miserable with time
Nothing she had experienced changed the
Pain that rained through her soul, her life
Filling her with a dread, a doubt, a darkness
That couldn't be lifted by any amount of kindness
Nothing on earth had prepared her for this
Silent echo of mourning, regret, torment

She was lost and felt so alone in her heart
Where the grief never permitted peace
Where the sorrow was never relieved
She was in pain and the pain never eased
But finally, in the twinkling of a smile
There came to her a second chance to believe
A second chance to know what it is to give
From a heart who has lived through the doubt
The throbbing, the sobbing of an anguish
That is so deep and dark it saturates the mind
With shadows that can't even be defined

Finally, she looked up to the Son
Who lights up the heart and soul
With His endless hope, faith and love
The tenderness that reminds us all
We have been blessed by the One
Who created us, awakened us to love
And poured out His spirit into our hearts

Without Him—where would we be?
There is no doubt He is the comfort and peace
That reassures and reminds that love
Is a treasure so alive, that despite the sorrow
We hold hands with the heart who knows us
As His children, the ones He gives
Inspiration and joy, love that is wonderous!

Praise Him—He is the One who reaches
Past all the pain and cheers us so we know
His love is alive, writing hope across our souls
Sending light so we can see—the way it is
When we allow Him to lead us with His grace
His insight and peace—the love that He is

Jesus is the answer to every need, each care.
With Him living inside your heart, there is no doubt
You know you have all your hope restored
Your joy and peace reconditioned
Your unconditional love is there with you
Flowing from the One who pours His love out
For your heart and soul to experience.

His Guiding Light

Bleeding music into
A heart who cries
Tears so gentle, so tender
They reflect the hope
So often called to mind
By one who knows
Lost love—left behind

Breathing light across
The soul who smiles
Peace and wonder, inspiration
Filled with grace, peace
Aliveness, a dance
Waltz of healing, stirring
Awake the flames
Of compassion, a brilliant
Whisper of emotion

Hushing the hysterical
Doubts and confusion
The disillusionment
Brought on by darkness'
Gloom, despair, distraction
The air of doubt
Curling around the murky
Stillness of a thought
Who bends with the weight
Of uncertainty, distrust

Baptizing these feelings
Who flow suspicion
Through the spirit
Sing of disbelief and dread
A blackness in hues of graying

Melancholy blended
In fear, nightmares diminishing
The beauty in a silence
The wonder in grace
The inspiration and enlightenment
Known by our sweetest praise

Praise Him through the worry
Let Him know your heart
Is always yearning for His touch
The warmth of a blessing
Filled with kindness and love
Strong enough to shine through
The shadows, lifting the dark
Inspiring the spirit to that fresh
Gentle feeling of pure, sweet hope

Let Him know you love Him
That He is the answer to each prayer
The whisper of a second chance
The song of inspiration and care
The guiding light who is always there

He Came for Us

He reached out His hand
And created even our hearts
With His light and love
He made us who we are today
Children who love and pray
His images whom He breathed
Life into—awakening
To the light of a new dawn
The glory of moon and stars
The joy of a heavenly sun

He filled the earth we live in
With light, love and laughter
Silencing the worry and fear
With a breath of His inspiration
Soothing the soul's despair
With wonder and joy and smiles
Sent to remind us all that
His love is enough to sustain us
His love is the greatest thing
We will ever know or find
His love is the answer to prayers
The kindness, the hope, the faith
That whispers through our lives
Inspiring, enlightening, inviting
Everyone to reach out and find
The wonder of a God who is alive
And welcomes our heart to ask
For the light to fall over the darkness
In rays of healing and fulfillment
Lighting the way for His grace
To prepare hearts to awake
With the joy pouring out inside
Always wonderous, always abiding

To encourage, inspire and delight
With His heavenly insight

He made us all to be His children
Alert to the yearnings He gives us
Pursuing a relationship with Him
A connection that is built on love
Abiding in the heart who knows He is
The light, the joy, the peace
The grace that gives us a chance
To believe in the One He gave
The One and Only SON, Jesus Christ
Who answers our heart's quest
For a Savior, a king, a friend
One who is the solution to our need
For salvation from the sin we bleed
From pores filled with angst and greed

He is the One who agreed to be
The Redeemer, the Peace, the Sacrifice
For the souls who know, without Him,
We'd be doomed to death and hell
Without a hope for the home we'll call
Heaven, the place He has prepared
For all God's children, the ones who know
He is alive and His Spirit lives on the inside!

Change

I like for things to stay the same
But changes come and I always exclaim
"Jesus, Help me—I pray in Your name . . .
Guide me past the worry and shame"

I miss the way things used to be
When I was young, alive and free
Joy rising in my heart, I agree
This was the time of miracles for me

I long for those moments of hope
Knowing Jesus would help me to cope
With sorrows that caused me to grope
In fear, feeling like I was hung on a rope

Refrain:

Darkness dims my soul's view
With colors black and blue
Reminders that I always knew
Without Him, I can't face the new

Changes like this are often burning
Dread and doubt are there, churning
Reminding me of the shift as I'm turning
From the familiar to the alien, undiscerning

Worries reflect my worries and strife
As I tremble with fear from their knife
Will I ever find hope in this new life
Where I struggle to adapt despite rife

Time presses me forward into the new
Guiding me to believe in the joy that grew
With a prayer answered by the One who
Loves me like His child, with a love so true

Walking His Path

Walking through this worldly land
Following my precious Lord
Wondering can I finally withstand
Because I'm following Him who is adored
By hearts and souls who understand
He is love sent from above with one accord
By the One who created all with His own hand

REFRAIN:

Lead me home, precious Lord
My sweet Savior, who is adored
Grace and hope sent to the world
To remind us that we can't afford
Losing this light, this love, this award
From the heart of One who won't be ignored
He is the answer to every prayer stored
Up in heaven, our home and reward

Lingering in my soul there is a light
Calling me to love with all of my heart
Filling me with a joy, a song, sweet insight
Beauty that reminds, His grace He does impart
With the wonder of a love sent—so bright
Freeing my mind of fears running rampart
It is this gentle peace of which I always write

Heaven can't imagine the wonder of such grace
Feelings alive, breathing sweet life
Through my feelings, poured over my face
Beckoning my soul to let go of worry and strife
Lean into the joy, the hope, the place
That won't discourage, cutting like a knife
Into the spirit of the one who knows His embrace

www.ingramcontent.com/pod-product-compliance
Lightning Source LLC
Chambersburg PA
CBHW071429150426
43191CB00008B/1091